ACCOUNTING REPORTS FOR MANAGEMENT

ACCOUNTING REPORTS FOR MANAGEMENT

Charles H. Mott

PRENTICE-HALL, INC. • ENGLEWOOD CLIFFS, NEW JERSEY

Prentice-Hall International, Inc., *London*
Prentice-Hall of Australia, Pty. Ltd., *Sydney*
Prentice-Hall of Canada, Ltd., *Toronto*
Prentice-Hall of India Private Ltd., *New Delhi*
Prentice-Hall of Japan, Inc., *Tokyo*
Prentice-Hall of Southeast Asia Pte. Ltd., *Singapore*
Whitehall Books, Ltd., *Wellington, New Zealand*

"This publication is designed to provide accurate and authoritative information in regard to the subject matter covered. It is sold with the understanding that the publisher is not engaged in rendering legal, accounting, or other professional service. If legal advice or other expert assistance is required, the services of a competent professional person should be sought."

—From the Declaration of Principles jointly adopted by a Committee of the American Bar Association and a Committee of Publishers and Associations.

Library of Congress Cataloging in Publication Data

Mott, Charles H
Accounting reports for management.

Includes index.
1. Managerial accounting. 2. Cost accountings.
3. Cost control. I. Title.
HF5635.M876 658.1'511 79-12752
ISBN 0-13-003004-X

Printed in the United States of America

ABOUT THE AUTHOR

Charles H. Mott has served as Controller and Vice-President for The L. Greif & Bro. Division of GENESCO and Treasurer and Chief Accounting Officer for Contee Sand and Gravel Co., Inc., of Laurel, Maryland. In addition, he has served such companies as The Pratt & Whitney Aircraft Division of United Technologies Corporation, The Davison Chemical Division of W. R. Grace and Co., and The Black and Decker Mfg. Co.

Mr. Mott is currently serving as consultant to Consumer Cost Consultants, Mt. Rainier, Maryland; Halco Products, Inc., Landover, Maryland; Tobin Pack. Comp., Albany, New York; and Litigation Support Corporation in San Francisco. He is presently Associate Professor in Accounting at San Francisco State University.

A Word from the Author

The economic downturn of the mid-seventies and the resulting sharp drop in profits re-emphasized the need for effective control of business operations. Cost control is the heart of managing for profit. In this book, not only the control of costs, but more importantly, the reporting of the effectiveness of those controls is emphasized.

Normal accounting reports, such as balance sheets, profit and loss statements, and cash flow statements are historical records of performance. But the reports included within this book, when used on a timely basis, result in decisions that will favorably affect the firm's current performance!

Each chapter of this book illustrates areas of costs that should be controlled and how to report on (read) whether the controls are effective. Within each chapter are sample reports which show the reader what, how and when to report. Readers will also find that as they read this book, methods for extending their present controls and reporting will be discovered.

If the areas, as suggested in this book, are subject to control and reporting, the firm's overall performance will inevitably improve. Frozen standard reporting will allow continuous tracking of product costs from introduction to discontinuance. The need to take advantage of technological change will be continuously before management, reminding them of the need to act. The result will be lower product costs and increased profits! Add cost reduction reporting; reporting on the costs of research and development, and all costs affecting products are subject to review.

Reporting on break-even analyses, audit reports of financial analyses, and reporting on incremental costs will support the tracing of all changes in the levels of discretionary or fixed costs. Managers will be able to adjust the spending on these costs to that needed to maintain profits.

The continuous reporting on forecasts, the use of zero base budgeting, the reporting on marketing programs, customer service ratios, and distribution sampling complete the control cycle. Reports on the effective use of the firm's total resources are available to management for review. Managers will know the effects of each of their decisions—continuously and immediately! The firm's managers can react to problems and correct sub-standard performance before it is too late and losses are incurred!

Using the complete set of reports included in this book, in addition to the usual monthly accounting reports, management has available the necessary information for complete financial and cost control of the firm's operating results.

CHARLES H. MOTT

CONTENTS

ACCOUNTING REPORTS FOR MANAGEMENT

Chapter 1

Frozen Standard Reporting: An Exacting Guide To Continuous Product Cost Control

WHAT HAS CAUSED A PRODUCT COST TO CHANGE? Was it a change in product material content or method of production, product redesigns, or poor cost control at some level of production? Variance analysis in most standard cost systems is extremely general, and it is difficult for management to determine cause and effect. Frozen standard reporting, as a supplement to the usual current and variation-from-standard reporting procedures, can be used to measure immediate changes in the unit cost of a product, so that the causes can be identified and action can be taken to stop unfavorable trends. Similarly, management can determine which products are contributing most to its profit objectives and can then make decisions which will shift sales emphasis to these products; or as an alternative, decide to use the cost advantage to decrease unit prices to gain a larger share of the market.

Setting up Frozen Standards and How to Use the Frozen Standards Report as a Profit Tool

Frozen standards are simply normal product cost standards which, by decision, are fixed at a particular point in time to be used as a comparison for future standards applicable to the same product. The frozen, or fixed, standard has the same component parts as current standard costs, and frozen standards are structured so comparisons can be made at more than one production part level, i.e., each assembly and sub-assembly of a product. Comparisons can be made for each cost category, including total direct labor costs per unit, direct materials, and variable indirect costs. Variable indirect costs are included because they are affected by changes in the method of manufacturing, therefore, indirect allocations will change. Frozen standards should, generally, be reported at the product level.

The frozen standard report is a comparison of current standards to frozen standards with the reporting of variations for each category and cost. In the comparison report, there should be a quantity field to show the estimated quantities to be sold in the current fiscal year. This is included to prevent management from wasting its time on products whose costs are changing, but which are not significant in sales volume. Conversely, a favorable change in the cost of a product when small quantities have been sold in the past could lead to a decision to put sales and marketing emphasis upon that product. A significant decrease in the unit cost of a product could result in a favorable price point and increased market share.

Example of a Monthly Frozen Standard Cost Report

Schedule A is a typical schedule showing current and frozen standards for a manufacturing organization in a consumer market. The report is printed monthly because of the continual and rapid changes in the costs of the products manufactured.

Fixing Standard Costs Provides an Immediate Measure of Changes in Product Unit Cost

The purpose of fixing standard costs is so changes may be easily monitored. The changes in the Cost of Goods Sold can be traced back to the particular products which caused the changes. The benefits are an immediate comparison of changes in product unit costs. Reporting through frozen standards highlights changes in product material con-

SCHEDULE A

FROZEN STANDARD COST REPORT AT THE END OF JANUARY 19XX

Product Code	Product Description	Direct Material	Direct Labor	Indirect Variable Costs	Total Variable Costs	QTY Sold LFY	QTY Forecast TFY	Code
2-11314	Widget ½″	100	50	10	160	100,000	110,000	C
		109	51	10	170			F
		−9	−1	—	−10			−%
2-11315	Widget ⅛″	109	55	11	175	75,000	77,000	C
		109	53	10	172			F
		—	+2	−1	+3			+%
2-11316	Widget ½″	110	57	12	179	250,000	270,000	C
	Variable	119	58	12	189			F
	Speed	−9	−1	—	−10			−%
3-11111	Widget	30	5	3	38	300,000	320,000	C
	Circular	30	5	3	38			F
		—	—	—	—			−%
4-11112	Widget	40	30	10	80	80,000	83,000	C
	Air ⅜″	42	29	11	82			F
		−2	+1	−1	−2			−%

CODE: Current Standard = C Frozen Standard = F

tent and this is especially useful when products are continually undergoing changes for reasons such as product acceptance, safety laws, durability, cost reduction, or innovation. The planning of Cost of Goods Sold for the next fiscal year should be as detailed as possible. Expected cost changes in the product line and expected unit volume should be incorporated into the plan. This permits a detailed comparison and follow-up to measure accomplishment or failure to accomplish the necessary cost reductions. The overall expectation is further delineated by product groups, and finally, by changes expected in particular products. The frozen standard cost report can be used to trace these expectations and determine whether or not plans were realized. If the goals were not realized, the failure can be traced to the specific products and, thus, the reasons for failure. Also, products can be identified in which there were unexpected changes. Plans which are dependent upon Cost of Goods Sold can be revised, and thereby management can react to the changes in its original plans. The impact of Cost of Goods Sold upon operations makes this approach essential to sound problem diagnoses and management. When managers receive the frozen standard cost report and see unfavorable changes occurring, they can take immediate corrective action.

Management can order a complete redevelopment program on a product, or can initiate research into simpler methods of manufacturing. As a result of the frozen standard comparison report, management could order a complete research effort into a new product or concept and could order a development program to redesign or change the material content of the product. An additional alternative is to make use of the available engineering talents to revise the method of manufacturing the product.

A Manufacturing Example

A manufacturer of sewing machines was not meeting its profit objectives. Investigation indicated the problem was an increase over plan in the cost of goods sold because of an increase in the cost of manufacturing Model A. The frozen standards for material, labor and indirect variable costs for Model A were compared to the current standard costs at the end of a particular month in the fiscal year. There was a significant increase in the current standards when compared to the frozen standards, particularly in the cost of material. It was also noted that this product accounted for 18 percent of total unit sales to date. The next step was to request an analysis or tabulation of the major assemblies that made up the sewing machine, such as the motor, mechanical parts, cabinet, and field case. From this tabulation it was determined that the material cost of mechanical parts had increased significantly. An inquiry was made of development engineering and it was decided to use a metal with less fatigue resistance, but which was more than adequate for the performance requirements of Model A. This change reduced the cost of manufacturing Model A.

From the detail presented in the frozen standard cost report, management will know and can contact the particular group where changes were initiated and can request an investigation of the causes. The analysis might show, as in the case of Model A, that a certain material cost increased. The manager can then ask those responsible for the purchase of the material why the cost increased and what alternatives are available. Or, the analysis might show that the cost objectives of a redesign of a product initiated by research and development engineering were not achieved. The frozen standard tabulation will lead to which particular group was responsible for the increase. On the other hand, the analysis might indicate a change in the manufacturing process which would mean a change initiated by application engineering. In either case, it allows management to understand the change and initiate whatever action it thinks necessary to modify the current condition or any indicated trends.

Monitoring the Cost Reduction Program

By reviewing the frozen standard cost report, management can immediately tell where a cost reduction program has been successfully implemented. If the cost reduction program is based upon reductions in product costs, management can monitor the progress and will know in advance whether or not the cost reduction goals have been accomplished. This knowledge could give management an opportunity to change the direction of its cost reduction program. It could be that during the current period the cost of a product changed because of maintenance, safety or some other modification; therefore, the product cost goals were not attainable. If a cost reduction is not being realized from one product, management can identify other areas in which to concentrate action to achieve a cost reduction. At worst, the manager can revise the cost reduction objectives.

The more detailed and better planned the objectives are, the more effective is the use of the frozen standard cost report. In setting the goals, a time frame for accomplishment must be identified. If the results are not occurring within this time frame, then alternative plans can be initiated and alternative opportunities sought. The product, group and section information contained in the frozen cost file make this alternative approach possible. However, the planning must be complete.

If profits were planned as a result of the redesign or just because of the profitability of certain products, management can see whether any changes in the costs of these products have modified product profit expectations. Then alternatives can be prepared.

From the frozen standard cost report, management can decide whether or not to shift its sales emphasis and objectives to products upon which cost savings are being made, or at least to those on which cost increases are not occurring. It may mean a complete shift in point-of-sale advertising as well as a shift in advertising emphasis to products where cost changes have made the most profitable gains possible. In addition, management can decide which products to discontinue or whether a price adjustment of a product is necessary during the fiscal year. Classifying which costs increased and which products can be discontinued requires consideration of many factors, such as the effect of a product discontinuance upon manufacturing costs and how much inventory is on hand. However, management will be acutely aware of those products that are contributing most to profits and those which are eroding profits, and they will have the option to consider prices if cost objectives are not being attained. For example, a cost reduction objective of a manufacturer of small tools was not being met. Management had assigned three months for the project of reducing the unit cost by $2.00 on a 200,000 unit per year tool. When the cost reduction was not accomplished within the time frame, the cost reduction goal was reassigned to a product with more possibility and the redesign and redevelopment efforts were redirected.

The market price or the price the market will bear must be considered before any price adjustment can be made. However, it is probable that competitors are facing the same or worse cost problems with similar products. Whatever product strategy is used, at least it can be formulated with the knowledge of the unit cost structure of the organization's product or products. Should unit costs decrease, management can decide whether downward adjustment in price is necessary to take advantage of a volume increase and increased share of market or whether prices will be maintained and profits increased because of the reduction in product cost.

Other Uses for the Application of Frozen Standard Reporting

1. *Evaluating Make or Buy Decisions.* The current versus frozen standard report has also proved useful for evaluating make or buy decisions. Often, in these decisions, manufacturing capacity is available and no increase in fixed costs will result from a make decision. The important issues are whether the vendors' variable costs plus profit are equal to or less than internal variable costs. This report not only lists current standards, but will indicate the trend from some point in time in the recent past. This trend, coupled with the other assumptions used in the analysis, will result in a more rational decision. This comparison can be made at the part level or whatever level is compatible with the decisions to be made.

2. *Use as a Competitive Tool.* The frozen standard report is also useful as a competitive tool. If the change in the costs of a product is the result of a safety redesign or a change in the basic material cost of some component of the product, it will be reasonable to assume competitors face the same problem. This information can be used or passed on to the marketing division to gauge competitors' reactions. From this, management can see whether competitors are willing to absorb the cost, increase prices, change the component parts of their products, etc. This does not necessarily mean that management will react in the same way as competitors. As a matter of fact, it might be advantageous to react differently. It is useful to gauge competitors' reactions so management can revise their own strategy or at least make their decisions based on the knowledge of what the assumed reaction of the competition has been.

It may be possible, even though the cost objectives are being met, to further improve performance, based upon the information contained in the frozen standard report. This report can also be used to look to the future if for some reason cost objectives cannot be met. If a product cost has been increasing and continues to increase, although not seriously in the current year, plans to replace that product in the future can be made.

Examples of Cost Savings Through the Use of Frozen Standard Reporting

As a result of the availability of the information contained in the frozen standard cost report, one manufacturer decided to study the method of constructing parts for its product. The trend toward higher costs as indicated by the report was offset by the manufacturer's decision to use powered metal parts as a substitute for castings and stampings. The change brought the cost of the product down and the savings were hundreds of thousands of dollars per year.

In another case, the continued high maintenance and manufacturing costs of a product resulted in, a complete redesign, instead of patchwork improvement. The result was that 19 parts were eliminated, the product was simplified, there was less maintenance, the source of power was more efficient because there was less leakage, and the savings to the manufacturer was approximately $3.50 per unit for that product which sold at the rate of 40,000 units per year. All of this resulted because of the trends indicated in the frozen standard report.

The Flexibility in Application of Frozen Standard Techniques

The application of the frozen standards can be tailored to suit the individual needs of a firm. The frozen standard report can be run on a computer or compiled manually. It can be structured to compare the frozen standards for the total product, the major assemblies or subassemblies. The frozen standards must be stored where they can be retrieved at any time for comparison to current standards. Once the standards have been decided upon, an identification code should be affixed, marking it as a frozen standard. In Data Processing, this can be done easily in the standard cost program. If it is a manual system, a code should be used, such as an "f" or a "p" or some designation that will prevent the standard from becoming confused with a current standard.

The standard is chosen at a point in time, such as the end of a fiscal year. Changes to standards take place continually within any time period; however, usually at the end of a fiscal year, all changes in product cost that have been initiated can be captured and a valid standard for each product then exists. The use of frozen standards will be dependent to some degree upon how efficient the entity's current standard cost system is. If standards are infrequently revised and a lot of effort is put into time-consuming and often lagging variance analysis, it may be worthwhile to concentrate on a more timely revision to current standards. Because of the value of the frozen standard cost report as a decision-making tool, there is pressure to keep the standards as current as possible so that meaningful comparisons can be quickly and easily made.

Frozen Standards—an Impetus to Keep Current Standards "Current"

If current standards are revised on a timely basis, the use of frozen standards becomes more practical. This implies that the industrial engineering or time study area which updates the standards is revising standards on a rapid and current basis. Management must be certain that these updates are being input to the standard cost system. Management can no longer tolerate the failure to revise standards as processes and designs change. The frozen standard cost reporting requires an efficient and effective application of standards changes and standard cost procedures.

Because it can, and does, happen that the update of the current standards is not input to the system because of difficulties in the computer input area, it could then be argued that one of the benefits of the use of frozen standards is the pressure that is brought on the group that maintains standards and on the information processing group to be sure that frozen standards are compared with standards that are as current as possible.

The suggestion that standards be frozen at the end of the fiscal year does not mean that at the end of the year the standards are arbitrarily frozen. The best procedure to follow is to update the standards for known changes for the end of the first fiscal month following year-end closing. For reasons of timeliness of reporting and to expedite decision making, the current standard file should be cut off four days before the monthly closing date. This will allow the current and frozen standards to be compared, run and printed out to management in time for them to receive this with their month end reports. This will avoid delay and allow them to review the complete financial system at once. If there is a high cost of sales, they can immediately check the frozen/current standard report. There is a danger in that there may be a four-day lag in the standard updates; however, any significant and important changes in that period can be prepared to answer any inquiry that may result from the early printing of the standard report.

The Pyramid Approach to Comparison

The best approach for comparison is the pyramid approach. Total direct labor, total direct material, and total variable indirect costs can be compared with the frozen standard at the product level by sorting on the product code or unit number. With available data processing technology, parts can be coded by traditional functions or by some of the more recent methods of coding, such as classifying parts by part shape. The point is that management can decide what it will have available. The only limitation to the detail is the ability to code the parts, assemblies and operations, and the capability to pyramid these into components and products.

Depending upon the requirements of the organization, standards can be frozen for part costs, and if there is an in-process system in the factory, for any operations which are captured on the automated in-process system. Operation and department costs can also be included in the frozen standard report. In this way, complete detail is available to trace any problems. In addition to the summary reports, if all details were captured and the programming were done, inquiries could be made when searching for solutions to particular problems and this could result in a comparative print-out of the frozen standard at the end of the last fiscal year with the current cost by cost category, such as direct labor, direct material, indirect variable costs, etc. Then this could be further broken down into assembly, sub-assembly, and part. Some other breakdowns are:

1. *Direct material:* Sections where input to material costs originate and particular types of material such as bar stock, copper, titanium, etc.

2. *Direct labor:* This can include a breakdown of costs by department and within department operations. In this way, changes in the operations can be seen.

Once the basic computer programming has been done, a simple patch or program modification can be made to create reports for almost any type of information which management can use for decision making. As an example, managers might find it useful to know within which areas the historical savings and cost reductions have been made. The reporting package could include a summary of changes such as:

SUMMARY OF COST FACTORS AND OTHER SOURCES OF SAVINGS AND REDUCTIONS IN STANDARD COSTS

Amounts ($000)

Description	Current Month	Year To Date	Total To Date
Direct Material	$ 10	$ 15	$ 50
Direct Labor	$ 5	$ 10	$ 20
Indirect Labor	$ 5	$ 5	$ 15
Fixed and Variable Expenses	$ 5	$ 10	$ 25
Engineering Change Orders	$ 100	$ 200	$ 400
Changes In Equipment	$ 50	$ 100	$ 200
Manufacturing Process Changes	$ 200	$ 400	$ 800
Totals	$ 375	$ 740	$1,510

This type of summary report is useful for identifying areas within which the cost reduction effort should be improved and to emphasize areas where a needed cost reduction may be found! With the costs of program maintenance, however, the need for these detailed breakdowns should be weighed against possible benefits.

Comparisons When Product Lines Change

Difficulties could arise when products are dropped or new products are added, or if a product is completely redesigned. Then the question of comparability with the frozen standard becomes a problem. Of course, in that case, there is always the option to use engineering standards until experience is gathered with the new product. The basic data file should contain the development engineering section, the applications engineering section, and the plant and product division responsible for the production of the part, assembly or product in question. The programming should be flexible enough to permit inquiry and a response with all pertinent and applicable information available for management to take swift action.

In a society of rapid change, new products and product discontinuance can cause delays or losses of product cost information unless management is prepared to solve these problems. If a product is discontinued and not replaced by a similar product, the discontinued item can be purged from the file and held in an inactive file. If, however, it is replaced by a new, similar product, the frozen standard cost report should be input to the file of the new product. This is especially true if the marketing strategy is to introduce a "new" product rather than redesign an existing product.

To develop a frozen standard file for a product which is a modification of an old product, the standard costs of any components that are the same in the new product can be input to the system. The remainder of the frozen standard can be made from the best engineering estimates. In this way, frozen standards will be comparable to current standards when the product is introduced. From this point on, as changes occur in the product construction, a useful file will develop.

The Exception Principle for Reporting Changes

The frozen standard report can be issued to compare the frozen standards for the total product, the major assemblies or sub-assemblies. However, a better method of compiling this report is to have only the exceptions printed out for the managers to examine. It is also possible to use a coding system to denote the most important products in the line. Frequently, a product line consists of "A", "B", or "C" products: "A" products being a small percentage of the line, but contributing "x" percent of profits. A code should be used to delineate the most important products and have only changes in those products appear on the report. The manager can limit this further by deciding which product costs to have on the report.

By the exception principle, management can request an examination of changes which have occurred. The investigation can be assigned to the appropriate areas of the organization and does not necessarily have to be the responsibility of the manager who receives the final report. The optimum frozen standard cost system allows inquiry pertaining to a particular part or product. Should a manager know of changes taking place, he can usually determine the effect by making an inquiry into the frozen standard cost system. The criterion for selecting which exceptions should be run, and whether the report should be by exception, is the volume of changes expected. If it is a rapidly changing market with rapidly changing products, particularly in the consumer field, more frequent runs may be necessary and they should contain more detail.

Explanation of the Frozen Standard Cost Report to Management

While management should determine the content and timing of the reports, it is important that the first reports be explained to the manager by a representative of the cost area. The explanation should contain all details of what is in the report, where the report originated from, which parts of the organizaton have input to the report, and what decisions could be made based on the information contained in the report.

The frozen standard comparison report can be generated at intervals determined by management to be useful. Under normal circumstances, the report should be run no more than monthly. It could be started on a monthly basis and then run more or less frequently, depending upon the number of changes which occur during that period.

After initiating the system, experience will indicate which is the best approach for timeliness of reporting.

When the current/frozen standard report is first run, it would be best to run it at frequent intervals, even if profit objectives are being met or exceeded. The reason for this is that it will allow management to adjust to the report, to understand the techniques and methods for applying it.

Frozen Standard Reports Are Useful to Manufacturers—Large or Small

Frozen standards are especially useful for manufacturing organizations with many products. It might appear, at first, that the use of frozen standards would be limited to manufacturing organizations with many products. However, they are equally useful to producers of few products which are complex in nature and producers who fall between the two extremes. Manufacturers with product lines which contain many parts and sub-assemblies, even though there are few final products, can use the concept of frozen standards as a guide to managing their product costs. The determination of whether frozen standards are applicable or not is, of course, a judgment of whether or not the incremental costs of a frozen standard system can be justified by the savings or increased profits made possible from decisions based on that system. Because of the flexibility of its use, frozen standard reporting can be a tool to increased profits.

Chapter 2

Three Cost Control Benefits of Break-Even Analysis Reporting

WITHOUT KNOWLEDGE OF THE BREAK-EVEN POINT, managers are not aware of the degree of risk involved when deciding upon prices, manufacturing methods, or expense levels. As elusive as the break-even point is, an approximation of the directional movement of the break-even point can lead to decisions which will prevent mistakes and the concurrent decrease in profits. Although historical information may not recur in the future, it is often, under many circumstances, the best practical estimator.

The Benefits from Identifying Changes in Fixed Costs

Break-even analysis is a proven tool for making business decisions. However, the benefits of break-even analysis are often overlooked in the decision-making process. Traditional break-even charts are discreet and usually a one-time analysis of the firm as a whole. Because of the number of variables affecting the break-even point, it is often thought difficult to use in any other manner. However, the use of contribution margin instead of the traditional gross profit computations and the reporting of the break-even sales volume without the traditional chart is easier and can, therefore, be used more frequently. One of the prime benefits of break-even analysis is that by tracking changes in the break-even point emphasis is placed upon the effect of discretionary (fixed) costs upon profitability.

A Re-examination of Traditional Definitions of Costs

The optimum use of break-even analysis requires a re-examination of some generally accepted definitions of costs:

1. Variable costs are usually defined as those costs which change with a fluctuation in total physical activity. From the point of view of unit cost, they are relatively fixed, i.e., it takes a certain amount of variable cost to create each unit of production within normal production ranges. For example, direct labor is a variable cost when related to production activity. Direct labor costs will rise with increases in production and decline with decreases in production. However, when related to unit cost, the direct labor cost per unit of product is relatively fixed.

2. Total fixed (discretionary) costs are defined as costs which do not vary with changes in total output. Regardless of the level of production, the amount of fixed costs remains relatively stable. On the other hand, fixed costs do vary per unit of production because of the fluctuations in production activity. Some examples of fixed costs are depreciation of buildings, leases for offices and production facilities and some parts of management costs.

3. The last traditional category of costs is semi-fixed or semi-variable costs. These costs can change from variable to fixed or vice versa, depending upon the level of production activity. For example, semi-fixed costs remain constant with the level of production until production increases to a certain point; then they change and become variable. Or, semi-variable costs usually vary with production until a level is reached at which they become fixed. These costs never vary directly with a change in physical production. In other words, they do not respond as directly to changes in volume as variable costs and they are not as stable in relation to volume changes as fixed costs.

There are a number of disadvantages to categorizing costs by traditional definitions. The implication of the usual interpretation of fixed costs conflicts with reality. There are costs which are relatively fixed over certain ranges of decision making, such as depreciation of assets or a lease on a building, but no cost is completely fixed. Underlying the use of the term fixed is a time frame. In the economists' definition of long run, no costs are fixed. In short run, it may be convenient to categorize some costs as fixed. However, there are some difficulties with this approach; for example, at what point is one's business operating in the short run; is there a point where short and long run intermingle? Should a new building be built which would increase fixed costs or should a building be sold or a lease renegotiated? Without knowledge of the full effect, this decision is impossible to make on a rational basis!

Although convenient in theory, economic definitions of cost do not help the practical businessman to know at what point in time he is operating and when or if he should attempt to influence the so-called fixed costs. A better application of terminology for non-variable costs is to look at all costs as being changeable. Decisions of management can change any costs. Even the relative fixed nature of the cost of a lease may be questionable when the bankruptcy of the tenant is a possibility or if the landlord, having no other solution, violates a lease agreement. It is convenient to look at all costs that vary with changes in volume of production differently from those that must be changed consciously, based upon assumptions other than production activity. The reason for looking at non-variable costs differently is there are no forces in the organization that will automatically respond to changes in activity and adjust these costs. The costs that are directly related to activity will be adjusted almost automatically when that activity changes. If not, the managers responsible know they will be questioned. On the other hand, for costs which are not directly related to production, the need for changes are harder to identify and it is difficult to decide upon alternatives when a change is necessary.

Generally, the criterion used by management to change variable costs is a variation in physical production. On the other hand, the so-called semi-variable, fixed or semi-fixed costs are not changed simply because the physical production has changed. These costs must be continually examined and consciously changed by a management judgment and by making a decision. For practical purposes, then, the term "discretionary" is more descriptive of these costs. In this way, all costs other than those that vary directly with the physical volume of production can be classified as discretionary. Management must look at each of these discretionary costs when production changes to determine whether or not they should take action to modify these costs. Management must apply judgment to determine whether the change in production warrants an alteration of discretionary costs. By categorizing costs which are borderline, or which are semi-variable, as discretionary costs, they can be examined in relation to changes in production activity, along with costs which are more fixed.

Break-even analysis highlights the effect of non-variable or discretionary costs upon volume and emphasizes the effects of management decisions upon these discretionary costs. This implies that break-even analysis can be used to audit the reaction or the performance of managers who must decide upon the need for these fixed costs. As the break-even point changes in an upward direction, management can ask those responsible if all discretionary costs have been reviewed and what decisions were made to control these costs.

> In 19XX, a major automobile manufacturer undertook a program of reducing its fixed costs for the prime purpose of reducing its break-even sales volume and increasing its margin of safety. Break-even points were calculated for each plant and profit center. Then a major effort to reduce the fixed expenses in each of these centers was undertaken. The break-even points were recalculated for each center and the results indicated a reduction in the overall company break-even point from approximately 250,000 units per year to approximately 230,000 units.

Break-Even Analysis Emphasizes the Effect Upon the Margin of Safety of Costs That Do Not Vary Directly with Volume

Historically, management has been concerned with indirect or overhead costs and whether value is being received from resources expended for these costs. The usual approach to measuring these costs is a comparison with the same costs of a prior period or on some budgeted basis. This does not sufficiently emphasize the effect of costs on the operations of a business entity. Break-even analysis and the use of the break-even point emphasizes the direct effect of these costs upon the margin of safety and therefore the profitability of the corporation.

The margin of safety is the difference between current volume and break-even volume which is directly affected by changes in discretionary costs. Management, by looking at the trend in the margin of safety, can see the risk involved when making particular decisions. Increases in discretionary costs or drops in volume without corresponding decreases in discretionary costs will reduce the margin of safety (raise the break-even point). From the information provided, managers can take corrective action and investigate why the margin of safety has decreased. Comparative budget analysis will not disclose this information. In addition, when an increase in discretionary costs is planned, break-even analysis will indicate the increase in volume required to cover that cost and still maintain current levels of profitability. For example, if the contribution margin percent were 10 percent, it would require a million dollar increase in sales volume to cover a $100,000 increase in discretionary costs. Such an increase in volume may not be possible with the current pricing strategy. A change in the pricing strategy may adversely affect profits. If this is the case, the expenditure should not be approved.

Break-Even Analysis Is Useful as Additional Input to Decisions Concerning Capacity Expansions or Contractions

Part of any decision for construction of new manufacturing or marketing facilities is the effect this construction will have upon the break-even point and the margin of safety. Decisions cannot be made solely by the effect of the decision upon the break-even point; however, an analysis of construction estimates to find the plan which best balances construction costs, variable costs and the break-even point is essential. It is important particularly in today's economic uncertainty, to attempt to find the optimum construction cost which will have the least effect upon the break-even point, and at the same time, accomplish the manufacturing cost and sales objectives. Break-even should not be, but is often, overlooked when a decision such as this is considered.

Break-even should also be a factor when deciding whether an existing facility is to be phased out or closed. Usually, the objective of a decision to shrink the size of a business is to reduce capacity. In making this decision, the facility or facilities with the highest break-even points should be high on the list of possibilities for closing. This is true because of the effect of the closing of those facilities upon the margin of safety. The greater the margin of safety, the easier it will be to reduce manufacturing and marketing operations or prices as volume declines. Break-even analysis will not be the only input to such a decision; however, it is often neglected when such decisions are made. One bit of caution should be noted at this point—decision makers should be aware of the effect of the deceleration decision upon all costs and should consider the trade-off between low unit cost with automation and the flexibility of a low break-even point.

> A clothing manufacturer found it necessary to review his business. This meant the need to reduce production capacity. There were two alternatives, to close an old plant where most of the cost was the result of manual operations or to close the newest and most modern plant which was highly automated. One of the inputs to the decision was the effect of the closing upon the margin of safety and thus the break-even volume. The extensive fixed costs required to operate the newer plant and the sales volume necessary to recover these costs were major considerations in the decision to close the newer plant and keep the older, more flexible plant operating.

The Effectiveness of the Break-Even Point

Because of the difficulty in evaluating the contribution to profits of discretionary costs, other measures are used to judge the need for the levels of expenditure on these costs. Based upon the directional movement of the break-even point, managers can decide whether to increase or decrease discretionary costs.

The single break-even point is based upon the assumptions that product prices remain unchanged, that the product mix is stable, that the relationship between productivity and variable unit costs has not changed, and that discretionary costs will not change. In reality, however, prices do fluctuate, the product mix changes, manufacturing methods change, and discretionary costs are unstable. Before managers can interpret the effect of a single break-even point, the break-even point has changed.

Therefore, the trend of the break-even point is more useful. And based upon that trend, managers can increase or decrease discretionary costs to affect its direction. An examination of the nature of the break-even point assumptions reveals why managers must react quickly while continuing to investigate and identify a more permanent strategy.

For example: (a) a reduction in prices without any other change will raise the break-even point because the contribution margin will decrease; (b) a shift in product mix to less profitable products will raise the break-even point because it will reduce the total contribution margin; (c) a change in manufacturing methods will affect the amount of variable costs in each unit of product. If the amount of variable costs is increased, the break-even point will rise, if the amount decreases the break-even point will decrease. The reason the break-even point changes is the effect the variable costs have upon the contribution margin; and (d) an increase in discretionary expenses will raise the break-even point because it will require more contribution margin to recover the amount spent on the discretionary expenses.

For the convenience of the analysis in the last paragraph, it was assumed that each assumption changed independent of each other assumption and that when one assumption changed the others remained constant. In fact, this is not possible. Simultaneous changes are occurring continuously in most, if not all, of the assumptions underlying break-even analysis. Managers cannot await further analysis. Prudent management may require an immediate reaction even if that reaction is to arbitrarily reduce discretionary costs. A firm must survive unfavorable trends in its break-even point in order to reverse them!

Methods for Computing the Break-even Point

One very effective method for computing the break-even point is regression analysis. Regression analysis is generally more precise than other methods. Within the techniques called "regression analysis" there is one which is known as multiple linear regression analysis. This technique is more accurate than other regression methods; however, it requires considerable study and more time than simpler methods to identify variables and to arrive at a formula applicable to the particular situation. That is, identification of which variables to include, whether there is any co-variation, whether the variables will be useful in the formula, takes time and requires much analysis. Therefore, multiple linear regression analysis is not recommended for general use unless there is time and the expertise is available to conclude such a study. Multiple linear regression analysis could best be used by very large and complex firms because it requires the investment of large sums to refine and identify the formula of best fit.

Simple linear regression analysis is less accurate than multiple linear regression analysis; however, it requires less time and is recommended because, generally, it can be adopted without the need for a major study. Under practical conditions, the assumption underlying the break-even point can change quickly. The easy application of the simple linear regression analysis fits these conditions very well. However, when using either simple linear or multiple linear regression analysis, it is best, if possible, to use a computer. The use of a computer saves time and permits more numerous computations under more varied assumptions.

EXHIBIT 1

SIMPLE LINEAR PROGRESSION ANALYSIS APPLIED TO BREAK-EVEN ANALYSIS

Computation of a Break-Even Point for a Wholesale Division of a Manufacturing Company on a Computer

The linear regression formula is $y = a + bx$. Y is the dependent variable; a is the constant and x is the independent variable. In the following case, y is total expenses, a will equal fixed expenses and x is the units sold during the time period in which the expenses were incurred. The computations included below are based upon 18 months historical data. The data will be input into a computer time sharing terminal.

The computer will ask:

"Enter number of observations"

Enter: 18

"Enter number of observations — independent and dependent"

Enter: 2

"Enter number of selections you want to run"

Enter: 1

"Enter y then x value for each observation"

Enter: 1,3,686,000, 60,500
2,4,352,000, 74,600
3,5,587,000, 95,600
4,3,114,000, 51,000
5,4,131,000, 72,000
6,5,649,000, 102,000
7,5,329,000, 94,600
8,5,257,000, 91,800
9,6,098,000, 107,600
10,2,266,000, 36,200
11,4,760,000, 90,000
12,4,080,000, 64,000
13,4,702,000, 72,200
14,4,906,000, 80,900
15,4,079,000, 62,100
16,4,070,000, 63,100
17,3,737,000, 58,300
18,5,725,000, 92,300

"Enter 1 for table of residuals or 0 if not desired"

Enter: 0

The computer will then print:

MEAN	STANDARD DEVIATION	CORRELATION	REGRESSION COEFFICIENT
76044.44	19461.22	.9720	48.7046

STD. ERROR OF REG. COEF.	COMPUTED T VALUE	INTERCEPT
2.9456	16.5348	600231.000

The standard deviation, standard error of the regression coefficient and the computed T value may not meet desired standards for "best fit." However, because of the time involved to find the best data, this computation will suffice for approximately the break-even point. The significant data are the intercept which is the value or the monthly fixed cost amount, and the b value which is the regression coefficient or the variable cost per unit sold. The result is the following formula:

$$y = \$600{,}231 + \$48.7046(x)$$

Because the above data is monthly, it is necessary to convert this to yearly break-even data. The fixed component is multiplied by 12 and an average of 12 months of units sold is substituted for the x notation.

$$y = \$600{,}231(12) + \$48.7046(912.0)$$

The result is the approximate yearly cost by fixed and variable components:

$$y = \$7{,}202{,}772 + \$44{,}348{,}595$$
$$y = \$51{,}551{,}367$$

In order to compute the break-even sales volume, it is necessary to estimate an average year's sales volume for the units included in the 18 month's observations. That amount is:

$53,235,600

The contribution margin percent can now be calculated by dividing the yearly sales volume into the yearly variable cost and subtracting the result from 1; the remainder is the contribution margin percent.

$$\text{C.M. \%} = 1 - \frac{\$44{,}348{,}595}{\$53{,}235{,}600}$$

$$\text{C.M. \%} = 1 - .833$$

$$\text{C.M. \%} = .167$$

$$\text{C.M. \%} = 16.7\%$$

The next step is to divide the 12 months fixed costs by the contribution margin percent (converted to a decimal) to arrive at the break-even sales volume.

$$\text{B.E.} = \frac{\$7{,}202{,}772}{.167}$$

$$\text{B.E.} = \$43{,}130{,}371$$

The margin of safety can easily be computed by deducting the break-even sales volume from the current sales volume. Assuming the current sales valume is the same as the historical sales volume, the margin of safety is:

Current Sales Volume	$53,235,600
Deduct Break-Even Sales Volume	43,130,371
Margin of Safety	$10,105,229

To convert the margin of safety from dollars to units, the dollar margin of safety should be divided by the average unit selling price.

Even if a computer is not available, simple linear regression analysis can be done manually without an inordinate amount of clerical effort and time. It involves just a simple knowledge of how regression formulas are computed. All that is required to make the computation are a worksheet and a calculator. The simple formula could be used by most organizations, large and small, for input to decisions when break-even analysis is pertinent.

The use of break-even analysis might appear to be applicable only for manufacturing firms, but this technique can be equally useful for service organizations even if sophisticated data gathering methods are not available.

> For example, a professional architectural firm can protect its financial position and determine its margin of safety by computing its break-even point. In this case, Net Sales would be billings to clients by month and the "y" value represents total expenses. By applying the break-even formula, and the use of the manual method for computing break-even "billings," the firm can ascertain how much revenue (or number of projects) it needs to sustain its current staffing and related costs. When management sees that billings for the coming year will be less than are necessary to maintain profitability, they can choose between such alternatives as more actively seeking new projects, reducing overhead costs, or laying off employees. These decisions can be made with the knowledge of how much reduction is necessary or how much new work is required. Since the costs of bidding on new projects can be expensive, a knowledge of the break-even point can aid the owner of the firm in deciding how much the revenue from the project would offset the costs incurred.

In addition, if billings decline, management can know how long it will be before it might be necessary to lay off any employees. This can save the costs of laying off professional employees and hiring new employees again if billings should increase within a few months.

EXHIBIT 2

MANUAL COMPUTATIONS OF BREAK-EVEN POINT

The manual regression formula for computation of the break-even point is the same as the computer method. However, the manual method involves more clerical work. The formula is $y = a + bx$. Y is total expenses, b is variable cost per unit and x is units sold.

The example below is based upon 12 months data for a clothing manufacturer. The first column is the sales volume in thousands of dollars. The second column is unit sales in thousands of units. This column is also the x value in the regression formula. The next column is total expenses in thousands of dollars — the y values. The next two columns must be computed to arrive at the a and b values in the formula. They are the multiplication of x times y and x squared, respectively.

Month	Net Sales	X Sales Units	Y Expenses	XY	X^2
1	5,970	99.7	5,522	550,543.4	9,940.09
2	4,799	81.3	4,507	366,419.1	6,609.69
3	3,915	66.3	3,777	250,415.1	4,395.69
4	2,669	46.1	2,762	127,328.2	2,125.21
5	4,304	76.6	4,115	315,209.0	5,867.56
6	5,539	98.8	5,218	515,538.4	9,761.44
7	3,968	71.6	3,858	276,232.8	5,126.56
8	3,604	66.1	3,491	230,755.1	4,369.21
9	4,489	80.6	4,301	346,660.6	6,496.36
10	1,969	35.2	2,173	76,489.6	1,239.04
11	4,796	81.0	4,523	366,363.0	6,561.00
12	4,128	64.7	3,919	253,559.3	4,186.09
Total	50,150	868.0	48,166	3,675,513.6	66,677.94

The next step in the manual computation is to compute the b value. The formula for this computation is:

b = (The sum of the x's) times (The sum of the y's) minus (the number of observations — months) times (the sum of the x's times the y's) divided by (the sum of the x's squared) minus (the number of observations — months) times (the sum of the x's squared) or expressed algebraically

$$\frac{\Sigma X \Sigma Y - N \Sigma X Y}{(\Sigma X)^2 - N \Sigma X^2}$$

The values taken from the table above result in the following:

$$b = \frac{(868.0)\,(48{,}166) - (12)\,(3{,}675{,}513.6)}{(868.0)^2 - (12)\,(66{,}677.94)}$$

$$b = \frac{41{,}808{,}088.0 - 44{,}160{,}163.2}{753{,}424.00 - 800{,}135.28}$$

$$b = \frac{-2{,}298{,}075.2}{-46{,}711.28}$$

$$b = \$49.20$$

The formula for computing the *a* (constant) value is as follows:

a = The mean (average) of y minus the b value times the mean (average) of x.

or $a = \bar{y} - \overline{bx}$. The mean of $\bar{y}$ is computed by dividing the total of the y column \$48,166 by the number of observations (months) — 12. The average is 72.3. Therefore,

$$a = 4{,}013.83 - (49.20)\,(72.3)$$

$$a = 4{,}013.83 - 3{,}558.64$$

$$a = 455.19$$

For yearly data $a = 455.19 \times 12$ or 5,462.28.

To check the computations, the computed values are inserted in the original formula and checked to the total of the *y* (expense) column.

$$y = a + bx$$

$$y = 5{,}462.28 + (49.20)\,(868.0)$$

$$y = 5{,}462.28 + 42{,}705.60$$

$$y = \$48{,}167.88$$

Before these values can be used for computation of the break-even point, the degree of correlation should be computed. In addition, it is of value to know the degree to which the dependent variable is determined by the independent variable. This can be measured by the coefficient of determination which is computed as follows:

1. Use the values for a and b computed above and insert the actual units shipped for months one through twelve. The result is y_c or the computed y value.

2. The actual computations are:

	$y_c = a + bx$	y_c
1	455.19 + 49.20 (99.7) =	5360.43
2	455.19 + 49.20 (81.3) =	4455.15
3	455.19 + 49.20 (66.3) =	3717.15
4	455.19 + 49.20 (46.1) =	2723.31
5	455.19 + 49.20 (76.6) =	4223.91
6	455.19 + 49.20 (98.8) =	5316.15
7	455.19 + 49.20 (71.6) =	3977.91
8	455.19 + 49.20 (66.1) =	3707.31
9	455.19 + 49.20 (80.6) =	4420.71
10	455.19 + 49.20 (35.2) =	2187.03
11	455.19 + 49.20 (81.0) =	4440.39
12	455.19 + 49.20 (64.7) =	3638.43

3. Subtract the mean of the y values ($\bar{y}$) from the computed y's (y_c).

4. Square the differences computed in three above $(y_c - \bar{y})^2$.

5. Subtract the mean of the y's ($\bar{y}$) from the actual y values $(y - \bar{y})$.

6. Then square the results of the computation in five above $(y - \bar{y})^2$.

7. The actual computations are included below:

	$(y_c - \bar{y})$	$(y_c - \bar{y})^2$	$(y - \bar{y})$	$(y - \bar{y})^2$
1	1,346.60	1,813,331.56	1,508.17	2,274,576.75
2	441.32	194,763.34	493.17	243,216.65
3	(296.68)	88,019.02	(236.83)	56,088.45
4	(1,290.52)	1,665,441.87	(1,251.83)	1,567,078.35
5	210.08	44,133.61	101.17	10,235.37
6	1,302.32	1,696,037.38	1,204.17	1,450,025.39
7	(35.92)	1,290.25	(155.83)	24,282.99
8	(306.52)	93,954.51	(522.83)	273,351.21
9	(406.88)	165,551.33	287.17	82,466.61
10	(1,826.80)	3,337,198.24	(1,840.83)	3,388,655.09
11	426.56	181,953.43	509.17	259,254.09
12	(375.40)	140,925.16	(94.83)	8,992.73
Total		9,422,599.70	.04	9,638,223.68

8. Compute the coefficient of determination which is the sum of the computed y's minus the mean of y squared divided by the actual y values minus the mean of the y values and this difference is squared, as follows:

$$d = \frac{\Sigma(y_c - \bar{y})^2}{\Sigma(y - \bar{y})^2}$$

$$= \frac{9422599.70}{9638223.69}$$

$$= .977$$

9. The correlation coefficient is the square root of the coefficient of determination computed as follows:

$$r = \sqrt{d}$$

$$r = \sqrt{.977}$$

$$r = .9885$$

Both the correlation coefficient and the coefficient of determination are large enough (over 90%) to assume the relationship between the variables is statistically valid.

To compute the break-even volume, the marginal contribution or contribution margin percent must be determined. This percent is computed by dividing the variable expenses by the volume and subtracting this result from one.

$$\text{Contribution Margin Percent} = 1 - \frac{\text{Variable Expenses}}{\text{Actual Volume}}$$

$$= 1 - \frac{(\$49.20 \times 868.0 \text{ units})}{\$50{,}150 = 12 \text{ months value of shipments}}$$

$$= 1 - \frac{\$42{,}705.6}{\$50{,}150.0}$$

$$= 1 - .8515$$

$$= .1485$$

$$= 14.85\%$$

For computing the break-even volume, the contribution margin percent is converted to a decimal and divided into a year's fixed expenses as follows:

$$\text{Break-even} = \frac{\text{Fixed Expenses (12)}}{\text{Contribution Margin}}$$

$$= \frac{\text{a value times (12)}}{\text{Contribution Margin}}$$

$$= \frac{(\$455.19)\ (12)}{.1485}$$

$$= \frac{\$5462.28}{.1485}$$

$$= \$36{,}783{,}030 \text{ Break-Even Volume}$$

Time Series Analysis

Time series analysis is another method that can be used for estimating the break-even point. If reliable cost/production relationships are not available, time series is the most useful. If it is only possible to estimate that production has changed over a period of time, time series analysis will relate changes in expenses to the variable time. By this method, the "a" value will become the fixed portion and the "x" value will be the variable portion. The formula for time series is $y = a + bx$.

Although time series analysis is not as accurate as regression analysis, under some conditions, it will be better than judgment. Time series is particularly useful where exact production figures are not available. For example, if it is known that production increased or decreased over a certain period of time, the computation of fixed or variable components of expenses against that time period will be more useful than nothing at all. The assumption, however, must be understood and that is that reliable production numbers are not available and there is some knowledge of at least the direction of the movement of the firm's activity both in the past and in the future.

EXHIBIT 3

TIME SERIES

The time series approach is useful when no exact production data is available. If it is known that production increased over a certain period of time but the exact amounts of change are unknown, the expense or costs being analyzed can be plotted against a time frame and the fixed and variable components computed. It should be remembered, however, that this method, at best, will result in an approximation of the break-even volume. The fact that it is an approximation notwithstanding, it may be more useful than no knowledge at all.

For example, if we assume the following:

Year	Total Expenses (y)
1	$ 257,600
2	398,000
3	483,700
4	560,300
5	590,500
6	793,900
7	864,200
8	929,100
9	1,046,800
Total	$5,924,100

To identify the fixed portion of the expenses, the following must be computed:

Time (year) which is $t_o - t_n$ and the x value*	x(to—tn) times y (total expenses)	$(t^2_o - t^2_n)$ X
−4	−1,030,400	16
−3	−1,194,000	9
−2	−967,400	4
−1	−560,300	1
0	0	0
1	793,900	1
2	1,728,400	4
3	2,787,300	9
4	4,187,200	16
Total 0	5,744,700	60

*The middle year is t_o. If there is no middle year, the two central years become − 1 and + 1.

The formula for the computation is:

$$y = (a + (b\ (\text{x which is equal to t})))$$

$$a = \frac{\$5{,}924{,}100 - \text{Total Expenses}}{9 \text{ Total Years (number of observations)}}$$

$$b = \frac{\$5{,}744{,}700\ (\text{x times y})}{60\ (x^2)}$$

Making the computations, the values are:

$$y = \$658{,}200 + (\$95{,}700)\ (\text{t or x})$$

Therefore, using an assumed Contribution Margin Percent, either known or estimated, of 30%, the break-even point is:

$$\frac{\$658{,}200\ (\text{a or fixed expenses})}{.30}$$

$$= \$2{,}194{,}000$$

The Difference Method

There are a number of manual methods for computing the fixed and variable portions of expenses which can be used as input to the break-even analysis. One method is the difference method. This method involves subtracting the change in expense items of two different production levels. Also, the two different production levels are subtracted to find the difference or change in production. Then, this difference is divided into the difference arrived at from subtracting the expenses which determined the variable expense. The balance, or the portion of these expenses which did not change, is considered the fixed portion. Although this is a time-consuming method involving much clerical work, it may be the best or only method available under certain conditions, such as when a computer is not available or there are insufficient observations for computerization. The difference method is also more useful when the analysis is to be segregated into smaller units. In that case, data gathered for each expense may be too numerous for manual regression analysis and it would be less expensive and time-consuming to use the difference method.

The fixed portion thus computed can be summed and divided by the contribution margin percent to arrive at the break-even sales volume. If variable budgets are used, this method will not be as time-consuming as when such budgets are not available. Variable budgets already have the expenses separated into fixed and variable components. A more general method, such as regression analysis, could be used if such budgets are not available.

If the objectives of the analysis are simply aggregate numbers, then it is best to use regression analysis. Under these conditions, manual regression analysis is less expensive and not as time-consuming as other methods. However, if the objective is complete detail, then it is best to use the difference method. When analyzing individual expense items for purposes other than break-even, such as financial analyses or variable budgets, the difference method can provide an economical way of separating fixed and variable portions of expenses. Although regression analysis would be more precise, it requires a certain number of observations.

In summary, if the analysis is an aggregate analysis, it is more feasible to use regression analysis. The more detailed it is to be, i.e., break-even by departments, etc., then the difference method becomes more relevant.

EXHIBIT 4

THE DIFFERENCE METHOD OF COMPUTING FIXED EXPENSES FOR BREAK-EVEN ANALYSIS

Assume the following values for expenses and production activity:

Expenses	\$28,000	\$40,000
Production Activity	600,000 units	1,000,000 units
Change in Expenses		\$12,000
Change in Production		400,000 units
Variable cost per unit		\$.03
Expenses	\$28,000	\$40,000
Variable Portion (Producton × \$.03)	\$18,000	\$30,000
Fixed Expense	\$10,000	\$10,000

The fixed expenses can now be totaled and divided by the contribution margin percent to determine the break-even point.

The Naive or Graphic Method for Computing Break-Even

Another useful method is the naive or graphic method. For this method, prepare a graph with X (production or activity) and Y (expense dollars) axes (see Figure 1). Plots of the amounts of particular expenses (discreet dollar points) over a period of time can be placed on the graph and a naive linear (straight) line of least difference can be drawn through these points. The intercept of the line of least difference and the Y axis will equal the fixed portion of expense. This fixed amount can be summed with similar values for other expenses and used to compute the break-even point. This is a useful method when applied to disaggregate analyses; however, it is time-consuming and inaccurate when applied to large amounts.

The Judgment Method

Judgment is also a method for ascertaining fixed expenses and therefore the break-even point. The judgment method entails the visual inspection of each expense and classifying it as discretionary (fixed)

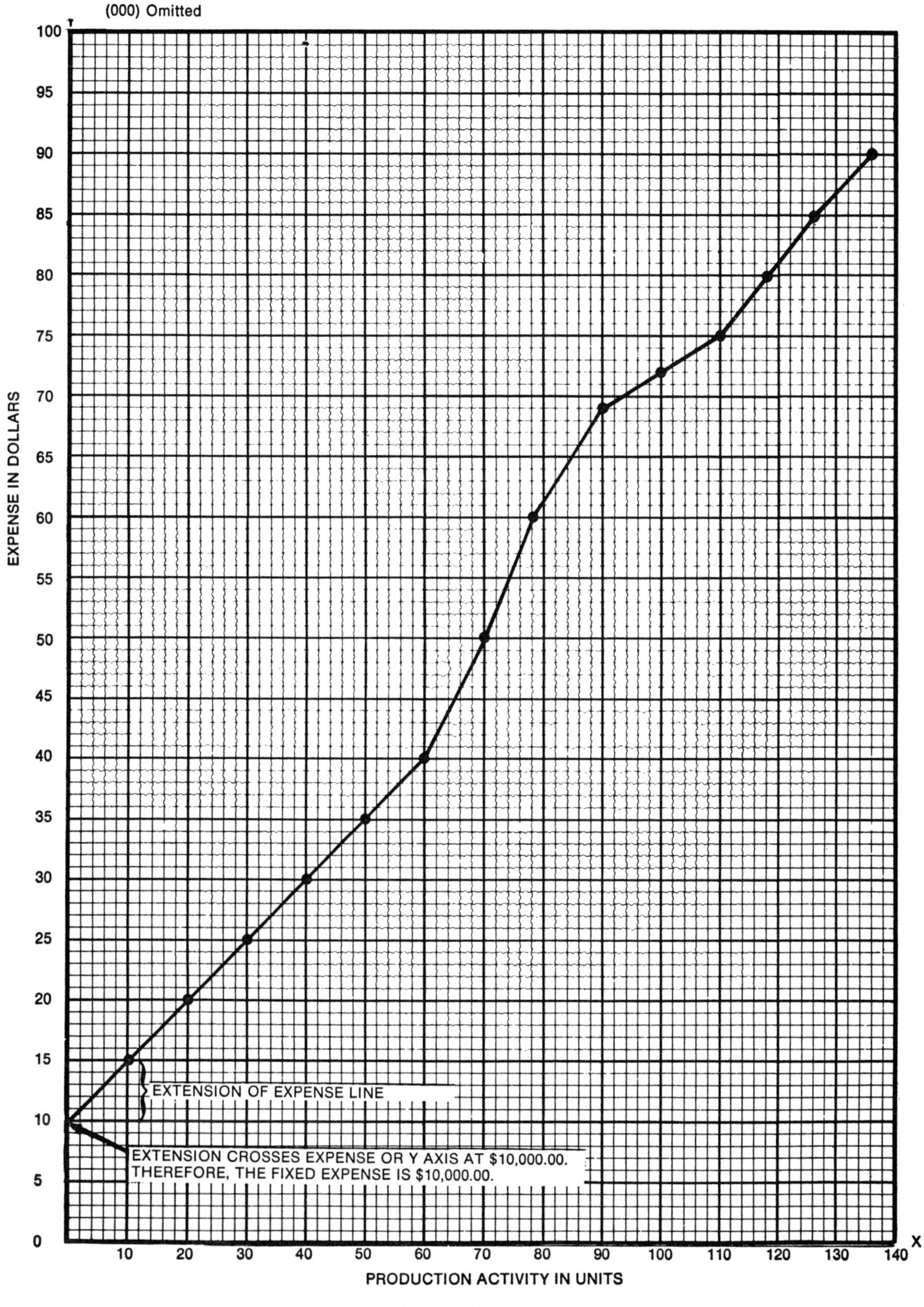
(000) Omitted
EXPENSE IN DOLLARS
100
95
90
85
80
75
70
65
60
55
50
45
40
35
30
25
20
15
10
5
0
EXTENSION OF EXPENSE LINE
EXTENSION CROSSES EXPENSE OR Y AXIS AT $10,000.00.
THEREFORE, THE FIXED EXPENSE IS $10,000.00.
10
20
30
40
50
60
70
80
90
100
110
120
130
140
X
PRODUCTION ACTIVITY IN UNITS

FIGURE 1

or variable, depending upon the judgment of the person making the review. This method is usually quite simple and only depends upon some knowledge of the expenses being reviewed. After they are classified, the fixed amounts can be summed and by dividing them by the contribution margin percent, the break-even point can be computed. Someone knowledgeable about the costs of a particular company, department or area could examine the expenses and classify them. For example, supervision could be classified as a fixed expense, timekeeping as a variable expense, security guards and watchmen as fixed, etc. Enough information could be gathered in this manner to prepare a break-even analysis.

With any of these methods, break-even charts can be prepared and the break-even point plotted as in the traditional break-even chart. Sometimes the use of the traditional chart is more feasible because it can be more easily understood and explained to some decision makers. Also, all the underlying assumptions should be listed in the chart, thereby making it visually possible to see that a change in any one of the underlying assumptions will change the break-even point.

How to Use Break-Even Analysis

Most text books and brochures written on break-even analysis show the break-even point as a single point and show one single chart. However, for practical use, a single point is not relevant. The break-even point depends upon the variable cost structure, the semi-variable or semi-fixed cost structure, the fixed cost structure, product prices and the level of activity, all of which influence the break-even point. It is very important to realize the effect of the relevant range of volume upon the break-even analysis. Although it is often claimed that expenses may change outside of a certain relevant range of production activity and the claim sounds simple, it is often very difficult to tell at what point one is operating within the relevant range or whether one is outside the relevant range. The relevant range is very difficult to define. Therefore, a break-even point computed at one level of production may be misleading because that point could be just outside or inside a range of production which will change the discretionary or fixed costs.

The simplest method of computation applicable to the circumstances is recommended because of the rapid changes in all the underlying assumptions used in break-even analysis, e.g., price discounting, escalating costs, including wage rates, changes in numbers and pay of supervision, innovations, etc. The gross profit computation is less complicated than the graphic method and takes but a few moments to compute. Because of the need to continually recompute the break-even point, this is the most practical method to use. Change is all that is certain in the conduct of business affairs, therefore, the continual recomputation of the break-even point makes break-even analysis a useful tool with which to rely for information upon which to base decisions. The recomputations should be done at least monthly. If this procedure is followed, changes in assumptions underlying the break-even point will be captured and a trend will develop. It is possible that changes in two assumptions would offset one another, however, any such phenomena will usually not last indefinitely and a monthly computation will eventually result in a trend upon which management can rely.

To summarize, the main advantage of the break-even point is that it emphasizes the effect of fixed costs upon profitability. It is important, however, to recompute it often and follow the trends and changes in underlying assumptions. The recomputations should be made at least monthly and can be used to: 1) plot changes in discretionary costs and identify trends in the movement of discretionary costs; and 2) identify the trend of the break-even point. A manager can see the effect of his decisions upon the margin of safety and, therefore, upon the total operations of the business entity. Both the trends and changes noted can be used as a basis for and an input to decision making about what action to take to constructively affect the profitability of the firm.

Chapter 3

How Post Audit Reports on Financial Analyses Increase ROI

AUDITS OF FINANCIAL ANALYSES ARE THE FOLLOW-UP of decisions which were already implemented. The purpose of the audit is to increase cash return on capital employed! The audit, which is initiated after the decision, must use the same method of analysis as that used to evaluate the decision. In most cases the analysis is of maximum discounted cash flow return. The purpose of the audit is to increase cash flow and maximize cash flow return on investments by learning whether or not the estimates from which the original analyses were made are accurate. From this, the organization learns where its estimating techniques are weak and establishes a record of which managers have the ability to estimate accurately. If any managers are consistently poor estimators, it will be apparent.

One difficulty with financial analyses, which must be overcome, is that the information required for the analyses is usually not available from the accounting records. This causes the need to study current operations to derive data useful for analysis. The post or "after the fact" audit of these analyses should follow, as closely as possible, the same methods of deriving the quantitative data as were used in the original submission.

The Purpose of Post Audit Reports of Financial Analyses

Frequently, the purpose and use of audits of financial analysis are misunderstood and, therefore, audits are not used to the extent possible. The sole function of audits of financial analysis is to maximize cash profits. The effect of these audits upon cash returns can be immediate. Audits can be scheduled flexibly, from a few months after the financial analysis has been approved to a final audit one year after the project has expired. For only the first financial analysis prepared by a firm is there a delay in the effect of the results from an audit.

From the first financial analysis forward, the audit will reveal variations from plan and where corrective action is needed! As financial analyses are reviewed for approval, reference to prior audits will reveal areas where adjustments should be made and where close follow-up is necessary! The conclusions of prior audits and the findings of audits in progress can also lead to a change in personnel if repetitive inaccuracies are traced to individuals. Audits have both a long-and short-term effect. Without audits of financial analyses, the organization cannot learn from its mistakes!

Examples of Financial Analyses Which Should Be Audited

Adding a New Product to the Line

If, for example, a manufacturer wanted to add a new product to his line, the first step would be to estimate the quantity of the product which would sell at a range of prices for a selected period. Usually, the farthest that management can see into the future is three to five years, therefore, a time period within this range would be selected. Then an estimate of the manufacturing cost for the product would be constructed and deducted from the most likely sales volume. In addition, the costs of any tooling required for the new product would need to be deducted. At this point, the cost of sales for the new product is developed and a gross margin can be computed. This analysis should also include an estimate of engineering development costs and variable (incremental) selling and administrative expenses, if any. After these costs are included, the operating income before taxes is computed and compared to the amount targeted or budgeted for the firm. Income taxes, which are usually based upon last year's rate, must be deducted before the net effect of the new product can be evaluated. The last step is to compute the yearly cash flow and the discounted cash flow return. This is the most useful and important measure of all, despite its implicit assumption of the need to invest the return at an equal or better rate than that earned on the new product. This project should then be ranked by comparing its rate of return with those of other projects. After approval, a copy should be placed in a follow-up file for audit. The audit should follow, as exactly as possible, the same procedure as the original analysis. Exhibit #5 is an example of a financial analysis of a new product prepared by a manufacturing concern. The financial analysis is followed by a subsequent audit.

The financial analysis was initiated because marketing identified a need for a new product. To the firm the possible benefits were increased market share and because of economies of scale, increased profits. The financial analysis was initiated to evaluate the contribution of the proposed product. The analysis confirmed that the product would contribute at an acceptable rate. To confirm the estimates used in the analysis, follow-up is initiated in the form of an audit. The results of the audit confirmed that the analysis was done right! The new product contributed a substantial cash return of 33.2 percent after recovering the investment required. It was a profitable and therefore successful decision!

Unfortunately, however, this is not always the case. One capital goods manufacturer financially analyzes all important decisions, but never conducts a post audit. Although the firm is profitable, there is no record of which part of the organization is making the most significant contribution toward these profits. Without an audit it is not known whether this is also the maximum profit which they can make. An audit would lead to correction of deficiencies in estimates prepared for financial analysis and assure investment in the most promising of the alternatives.

EXHIBIT 5

PRODUCT INTRODUCTION REQUEST
(Financial Analysis)

Financial Evaluation 3 Year Estimated Sales	Proposed Estimated $ Thous.	 %	Conservative Estimate $ Thous.	 %
Projected Sales	602.0*	100.0	451.5*	100.0
Estimated Manufacturing Cost	250.0	41.5	187.5	41.5
Tooling Costs	35.0	5.8	35.0	7.8
Total Cost of Sales	285.0	47.3	222.5	49.3
Gross Margin	317.0	52.6	229.0	50.7
Engineering Development Cost	22.0	3.6	22.0	4.9
Variable Selling and Admin. Expenses	8.4	1.4	6.3	1.4
Operating Income	286.6	47.6	200.7	44.4
Less Taxes	159.0	26.4	111.4	24.7
Net Income	127.5	21.1	89.3	19.7
Return on Discounted Cash Flow		31.9		25.9
Budgeted Operating Income		42.9		
Budgeted Net Income		9.9		

Comments:		
	Three Year Unit Volume	2,500
	Unit Cost	100.00
	List Price	245.00

*Net of Estimated Cash Discount of 1.75%

This evaluation illustrates the need for a two-point estimate; a most likely or proposed and a conservative estimate. The estimate used as the objective is the proposed. The conservative estimate is used as a measure of risk. In this case, both estimates exceed the budgeted operating income, budgeted net income and budgeted discounted cash flow (15.0%).

EXHIBIT 5

AUDIT OF PRODUCTION INTRODUCTION REQUEST
FINANCIAL EVALUATION AUDIT
(Audit of Financial Analysis)

Description Three Year Sales	Original Estimated Dollars	 Percent	Audit Results Dollars	 Percent
Projected Sales	$602.0	100.0	$710.0*	100.0
Estimated Manufacturing Cost	250.0	41.5	284.0	40.0
Tooling Costs	35.0	5.8	36.0	5.1
Total Cost of Sales	$285.0	47.3	$320.0	45.1

Exhibit 5 (Audit of Financial Analysis, continued)

Gross Margin	317.0	52.6	390.0	54.9
Engineering Development Cost	22.0	3.6	40.0	5.6
Variable Selling and Administrative Expense	8.4	1.4	11.4	1.6
Operating Income	286.6	47.6	338.6	47.7
Less Taxes	159.0	26.4	187.9	26.5
Net Income	$127.5	21.1	$150.9	21.2
Return on Discounted Cash Flow		31.9		33.2
Budgeted Operating Income		42.9		
Budgeted Net Income		9.9		
Unit Volume Two Years Actual, One Year Forecast		2,950		
Unit Cost		$96.27		
List Price		245.00		

*Cash Discount Taken and Expected for Remaining Year 1.8%

ANALYSIS USED FOR THE AUDIT WHICH IS CONSISTENT WITH THE ORIGINAL PROJECTION

1. The audit was initiated after the first two years of sales. Therefore, the audit included two years of actual data and one year of estimated data.

2. Gross Sales less cash discounts were spread over the three years as they actually occurred. Sales are treated as cash inflow.

3. The Standard Manufacturing Cost plus a percentage for variation from standard were spread over the three years in the same proportion as the units sold. The manufacturing cost is a cash outflow.

4. The Tooling Costs are treated as a cash outflow during the first year of manufacture which is usually the same as the first year of sales. As the tooling is amortized over the three years of producing the product, the tax shield is treated as income.

5. The Engineering Development Costs are cash outflow in the year prior to the first year of sales. The tax shield from the amortization of development costs is treated as cash inflow over the three years of sales of the product. (The current rulings of the Financial Accounting Standards Board regarding the expensing of development costs may change the timing of the cash inflow from the tax shield, but that is the only effect of the new rules.)

6. Variable Selling and Administrative Expenses are included as cash outflow in the three years of sales.

7. Income Taxes are considered cash outflow over the three years in which sales are made. (For a particular project it is impractical to allocate or defer income taxes. Therefore, they are treated as cash outflow.)

8. In addition, the working capital required for accounts receivable and inventories must be included in cash outflow prior to the first year of sales and included as cash inflow after the last year of sales. Working capital should be established as a percent of sales. Then the amount for the first year of sales can be included prior to that year's sales. Any change in the necessary working capital is included as cash outflow or inflow in subsequent years. The working capital is "returned" and becomes cash inflow after the last year of sales. For example,

a. Assume yearly sales as follows, Year 1: $100,000, Year 2: $200,000, Year 3: $150,000.

b. A Working Capital Ratio to Sales of 30%.

c. Working Capital Computation, Year 1: $30,000, Year 2: $60,000, Year 3: $45,000.

d. Application of Working Capital:

Years	0	1	2	3	4
Sales		$100,000	$200,000	$150,000	
Working Capital Flow	($30,000)	($30,000)	$ 15,000		$45,000

( ) Signifies Cash Outflow

9. Compute the discounted cash flow return.

Evaluating Investments in New Equipment

Audits of financial analyses also are used to evaluate the effects of investments in capital equipment. The financial analysis and the audit should be structured to include the gross purchase cost of the equipment plus the gross operating costs. This requires an estimate of material usuage, the direct labor costs of operating the equipment, and the costs of any contemplated overtime or shift bonus payments. The analysis must also include indirect labor cost, fringe benefits, materials and supplies and any other costs associated with the use of the equipment. In addition, the gross savings expected from the purchase must be approximated. These savings include materials, direct labor, overtime, shift bonus, indirect labor, fringe benefits, materials and supplies, and any other miscellaneous savings.

The estimates of both savings and costs should be prepared by year, with five-year estimates as the most practical limit because, for analytical purposes, it is assumed one cannot see beyond five years into the future. The next step is to deduct the gross yearly cost of the new machine from the gross annual savings to arrive at the net savings per year. The net savings must be reduced by the taxes on income which are computed from the latest available year in which income taxes were payable. The remainder is the net cash savings after taxes. Finally, the net cash flow and the discounted cash flow return are computed. The objective is a fast repayment of investment plus an incremental return.

The cash outflow is defined as (a) the purchase price of the machine which is included as an outflow in the first year. Then, (b) the net savings after taxes per year are increased by the yearly depreciation, the total of which is the net cash inflow, (c) the cash outflow is deducted from the net cash inflow to arrive at the net cash flow, and (d) from the net cash flow, the discounted cash flow return is computed. Based upon this return, the decision is made to authorize the purchase or disapprove the request. However, even though the purchase will result in a favorable return, it must be compared with other investment opportunities to confirm that it will return more than other alternatives before the purchase can be authorized.

Assuming the purchase is authorized, an audit of the actual results achieved must be scheduled. The audit should commence at the latest, at the end of the first year of operation to evaluate the progress against the original plan. There should be an additional audit halfway through the project, i.e., at the end of two and one-half years. Then there should be a final audit including the issuance of a formal report at the completion of the project or at the end of the fifth year of operation. Exhibit 6 is an example of an analysis of a proposed purchase of a machine including the results of a post audit.

The purchase of the machine was proposed by the manufacturing division to increase the return on invested capital for the operation which the machine performs. The machine currently performing these operations is obsolete. The new machine, it is contemplated, will increase the firm's profitability. The estimated discounted cash flow return from the purchase of the new machine is 38.2 percent which is 18.2 percent greater than the return required for investments in machinery. An analytical summary was prepared for evaluation of the proposal and a subsequent audit. The audit indicated a return of 39.3 percent which was 19.3 percent greater than expected or budgeted. The result was an increase in the effective use of money invested in the business.

> One manufacturer of soft goods prepares financial analyses for projected projects, but does not audit them. Periodically, each projection is redone until the period of implementation has almost passed. Then no further analyses are prepared. This results in a complete lack of information about the success of any analysis because it is impossible to audit for all the analyses prepared for a project. This firm expends resources for financial analysis without even knowing whether the results expected are being realized. This organization has incurred losses in the past and does not know whether any of the decisions which have been analyzed have contributed to or have minimized the losses sustained.

EXHIBIT 6

ESTIMATED SAVINGS FROM PURCHASE OF MACHINE

Proposal To Purchase Machine A
Estimated Return **(000)**

Costs To Operate Machine A

	Year 1	Year 2	Year 3	Year 4	Year 5	Total
Material Cost	$10.0	$10.0	$10.0	$10.0	$10.0	$ 50.0
Direct Labor Cost	36.0	36.0	36.0	36.0	36.0	180.0
Indirect Labor Cost	9.0	9.0	9.0	9.0	9.0	45.0
Estimated Overtime	1.0	1.0	1.0	1.0	1.0	5.0
Shift Bonus	2.0	2.0	2.0	2.0	2.0	10.0
Fringe Benefits (¼)	11.0	11.0	11.0	11.0	11.0	55.0
Supplies	1.0	1.0	1.0	1.0	1.0	5.0
Utilities	3.0	3.0	3.0	3.0	3.0	15.0
Maintenance and Repairs	4.0	4.0	4.0	4.0	4.0	20.0
Total	$77.0	$77.0	$77.0	$77.0	$77.0	$385.0

EXHIBIT 6 (Continued)

ESTIMATED SAVINGS FROM PURCHASE OF MACHINE

Proposal To Purchase Machine A
Estimated Return (000)

Savings From Installation of Machine A (Gross)						
Material Savings	0	0	0	0	0	0
Direct Labor	90.0	90.0	90.0	90.0	90.0	450.0
Indirect Labor	45.0	45.0	45.0	45.0	45.0	225.0
Overtime	2.0	2.0	2.0	2.0	2.0	10.0
Shift Bonus	2.0	2.0	2.0	2.0	2.0	10.0
Fringe Benefits (1/4)	33.0	33.0	33.0	33.0	33.0	165.0
Other	1.0	1.0	1.0	1.0	1.0	5.0
Total	$173.0	$173.0	$173.0	$173.0	$173.0	$865.0
Net Savings Before Income Taxes	$96.0	$96.0	$96.0	$96.0	$96.0	$480.0
Income Taxes at Rate of 40%	38.4	38.4	38.4	38.4	38.4	192.0
Total Net Savings	$57.6	$57.6	$57.6	$57.6	$57.6	$288.0

Cash Flow						
Investment:						
Mach. & Equip.	$100.0	—	—	—	—	$100.0
Total (A)	$100.0					$100.0
Net Savings	57.6	57.6	57.6	57.6	57.6	288.0
Depreciation (10 years Straight Line)	10.0	10.0	10.0	10.0	10.0	50.0
Total Cash Inflow (B)	67.6	67.6	67.6	67.6	67.6	388.0
Cash Outstanding (A-B)	(32.4)	67.6	67.6	67.6	67.6	238.0

DCF Return 38.2%
DCF Objective (Budget) 20.0%

EXHIBIT 6 (Continued)

AUDIT OF ESTIMATED SAVINGS FROM PURCHASE OF MACHINE

Return From Purchase of Machine A **(000)**

Costs To Operate Machine A

	Year 1	Year 2	Year 3	Year 4	Year 5	Total
Material Cost	$12.0	$12.0	$12.0	$12.0	$12.0	$ 60.0
Direct Labor Cost	35.0	35.0	35.0	35.0	35.0	175.0
Indirect Labor Cost	10.0	10.0	10.0	10.0	10.0	50.0
Estimated Overtime	1.0	1.0	1.0	1.0	1.0	5.0
Shift Bonus	2.0	2.0	2.0	2.0	2.0	10.0
Fringe Benefits (¼) of Labor	11.0	11.0	11.0	11.0	11.0	55.0
Supplies	1.0	1.0	1.0	1.0	1.0	5.0
Utilities	4.0	4.0	4.0	4.0	4.0	20.0
Maintenance and Repairs	5.0	5.0	5.0	5.0	5.0	25.0
Total	$81.0	$81.0	$81.0	$81.0	$81.0	$405.0
Savings From Installation of Machine A (Gross)						
Material Savings	0	0	0	0	0	0
Direct Labor	100.0	100.0	100.0	100.0	100.0	500.0
Indirect Labor	50.0	50.0	50.0	50.0	50.0	250.0
Overtime	2.0	2.0	2.0	2.0	2.0	10.0
Shift Bonus	2.0	2.0	2.0	2.0	2.0	10.0
Fringe Benefits (¼)	37.0	37.0	37.0	37.0	37.0	185.0
Other	1.0	1.0	1.0	1.0	1.0	5.0
Total	$192.0	$192.0	$192.0	$192.0	$192.0	$960.0
Net Savings Before Income Taxes	$111.0	$111.0	$111.0	$111.0	$111.0	$555.0
Income Taxes at the Rate of 40%	44.4	44.4	44.4	44.4	44.4	222.0
Total Net Savings	$66.6	$66.6	$66.6	$66.6	$66.6	$333.0

EXHIBIT 6 (Continued)

AUDIT OF ESTIMATED SAVINGS FROM PURCHASE OF MACHINE

Return From Purchase of Machine A **(000)**

Cash Flow

	Year 1	Year 2	Year 3	Year 4	Year 5	Total
Investment:						
Mach. & Equip.	125.0	—	—	—	—	125.0
Total A						
Net Savings	66.6	66.6	66.6	66.6	66.6	333.0
Depreciation (10 years—Straight Line)	12.5	12.5	12.5	12.5	12.5	62.5
Total Cash Inflow (B)	79.1	79.1	79.1	79.1	79.1	395.5
Cash Outstanding (A-B)	(45.9)	79.1	79.1	79.1	79.1	270.5

DCF Return 39.3%
DCF Objective (From Financial Analysis) 38.2%

Allocating Expenditures

Financial analysis is also a very useful tool for choosing between the expenditure of resources for investment or for items of an expense nature. If, for example, the choice were between spending money for a new data processing system which would reduce the investment in finished goods inventory or to continue the current investment in finished goods, a sound financial analysis would provide the profitability data for the decision. Similar to the analyses illustrated in Exhibits #5 and #6, a five-year estimate is used. The estimate should include savings in inventory carrying costs and in interest from reducing the working capital requirements. The analysis includes the calculation of the discounted cash flow return on the investment. The return calculated is compared to the target return and returns from other investment opportunities. Then the decision is made to spend the funds either on this or some other project. If this project is chosen, a post audit is necessary. Again, there should be interim audits and at the end of the project, a formal report of the actual results achieved.

Exhibit #7 is an example of an analysis of a choice of this type and the subsequent audit of the results.

The data processing equipment provides faster reaction to inventory changes. Therefore, the inventory level can be kept lower. If more inventory is needed, a factory run can be scheduled in advance from the data provided by the automated system. In this case, the need is for a comparative analysis with an after-the-fact verification. The original analysis indicates an estimated DCF return of 56 percent. This exceeds the budgeted or desired return of 29 percent. However, as indicated in the exhibit, the actual results did not live up to expectations.

Audits of financial analysis are very effective for implementing cost control. If the audits reveal a continuous failure to accomplish the original objectives, the manager responsible can expect disciplinary action. However, its most immediate effect is the knowledge by those preparing analyses that they will be subject to audit!

EXHIBIT 7

FINANCIAL ANALYSIS
(000)

Choice Between a New Data Processing System or Continued Current Levels of Investment in Inventories

Facts

1. Installation Cost Of Data Processing System $300.0
2. Operating Cost $200.0 each year thereafter.
3. The inventory investment will be reduced by a minimum of $2,000.0

Calculations

1. Inventory carrying costs (including interest) are 30%, the savings from the reduced investment are (30% × $2,000.0) or $600.0 annually.
2. The costs are $300.0 the first year and $200.0 each year thereafter.
3. The computation of the projected discounted cash flow return.

Assumptions

1. The analysis will be carried out for the standard five years. (Again, based upon the assumption that five years into the future is a practical limit for human vision.)

2. The first year will result in only one-half the normal annual savings being realized.

3. The target rate of discounted cash flow return is 29%.

Year	Cash Flow Inflow	Outflow	Net
1	$300.0	$300.0	-0-
2	600.0	200.0	$400.0+
3	600.0	200.0	400.0+
4	600.0	200.0	400.0+
5	600.0	200.0	400.0+

Discontinued Cash Flow Return 56%

EXHIBIT 7 (Continued)

AUDIT #12

Choice Between a New Data Processing System or Continued Current Levels of Investment in Inventories

AUDIT OF FINANCIAL ANALYSIS (000)

Actual Facts

1. Installation Cost of Data Processing System $400.0
2. Operating Cost each year thereafter $300.0
3. The inventory investment was reduced by $1,500.0

Calculations

1. The inventory carrying costs are approximately 30%, therefore, the annual savings are (30% × $1,500.) $450.0

2. The actual costs are as in items one and two above.

3. The computation of the actual discounted cash flow return.

Assumptions

1. The audit covered a period of five years from the date of initiation of the project.

2. The first year's savings actually were $338.0, which is ¾ of the annual savings.

3. The target rate of return remains the same as that included in the original analysis.

Year	Cash Flow		
	Inflow	Outflow	Net
1	$338.0	$400.0	$(62.0)
2	450.0	300.0	150.0+
3	450.0	300.0	150.0+
4	450.0	300.0	150.0+
5	450.0	300.0	150.0+

Discounted Cash Flow Return 31%

Audit Comments: The actual results failed to meet the expected results of 56%. However, the results exceeded the target rate of return of 29%. Because this project may have been given funding priority based upon the estimated rate of return, the reasons the savings and costs varied from expectations should be investigated.

The Nature of Financial Analysis

The benefits of audits of financial analyses depend upon the extent of the analyses themselves. Usually, the decision maker is faced with the need to determine the cash inflow and outflow. To compute these flows, it is necessary to rely upon estimates. The information required for such estimate is rarely available from the accounting records because these records are historically oriented, while decisions are forward looking. Therefore, judgments and estimates are necessary.

Post Audits Can Increase Return on Investment

One benefit from audits of financial analyses is they will help the organization to invest resources for the largest possible return. The objective of financial analysis is to take advantage of internal leverage, i.e., to make the most return from the current investment.[1]

One highly profitable company subjects all its important decisions to financial analysis and audit. Whenever a manager within the firm is faced with a decision which requires the use of significant amounts of resources, the decision is subjected to rigorous financial

[1] There is really no cash outflow for the use of existing facilities although they do have alternative uses. One method of treating existing facilities in financial analysis is to include those to be used as outflow at the beginning of the project and inflow at the end, in effect, burdening the project with the time value of the use of these facilities.

analysis and audit. Examples of such decisions include purchases of equipment, investment in new products, the use of such scarce resources as engineering or data processing or the incurring of major expenses.

The financial analysis must be completed before a decision so the manager knows the financial impact of the choices available to him. The decision may not always favor the greatest financial return as that indicated by the analysis. However, managers must know the financial implications of their decisions before they choose. For example, if the problem is whether to lower the price of a product in a certain market area or to invest in special promotions, the effect upon the corporation of this choice must be estimated in advance. A decision to seek certain marketing objectives rather than to earn the most return will be evaluated differently if it were to affect profitability by 20 percent than if the effect was 1 percent. The degree of risk is an important factor which must be considered when making a decision. More general examples of where financial analysis can be used to advantage are for capital budgeting decisions, make or buy decisions, lease or buy decisions, and for examining the trade-off between fixed and variable costs. Once a policy for financially analyzing decisions has been established, it is simple to develop a policy for audit of these decisions.

Cost control is achieved if the audits reveal that the objectives have been met, at least within reasonable limits. Those financial analyses that continually do not meet the required objectives will cause organizational change. However, the possibility of audit results in more accurate financial analyses than would be possible otherwise!

Post Audits Strengthen Future Decisions

Each audit will strengthen future analyses and thereby future decisions. The purpose of the audit should be to find the weaknesses in analyses and estimation, to emphasize the problems in projecting so the organization can correct these problems and prepare more accurate analyses in the future. If these audits are used strictly to discipline employees, the results will be disappointing. However, if they are used for organizational development and learning, for re-examining the decision-making process, as well as for disciplinary purposes, they can be most valuable and increase returns from investments. The comparison of actual results to expectations can also indicate where sufficient information is not available. Resources can be invested, if necessary, to make the needed information available. Such comparisons will identify sections of the company, divisions or departments, where consistently poor or consistently good analyses, and thereby decisions, originate. The results of the audit in these cases can be the promotion or retraining of personnel or an investigation of why some groups can estimate reasonably accurately while others cannot.

The matching of results with expectations can disclose problems in the methodology of estimating as well as in the methods used for constructing analyses. This may also point to weaknesses in the data collection and assimilation areas. Once these weaknesses are identified, changes can be made to generate more accurate and complete data which will result in more effective control of costs. When consistently applied, these audits can also indicate which managers within the organization are making good or poor decisions.

In short, audit results can lead to investigations of the causes of variations from projections.

> One hard goods manufacturer made a comprehensive audit of all financial analyses approved during three fiscal years. This audit included financial analyses of new equipment purchases, new product development, and improvements in business methods such as the increased use of automation. The actual results were within 5 percent of the estimates for the total of all projects undertaken during that period. This is an indication of the accuracy that can be achieved. It is proof that a well-defined method of evaluating decisions can cause profitable results. This manufacturer has his costs under control!

The Methodology for Conducting Audits of Financial Analyses

Audits of financial analyses should be conducted by that part of the organization which is the least interested in the results of a particular analysis. In manufacturing organizations with which the author is familiar, this is the financial division. The financial division's only interest is profitable operating results. Generally, it has no interest in a particular project and is, therefore, more apt to seek accurate information rather than information biased in favor of any particular project. The selection of who is to conduct audits is particularly important because the information necessary for an effective audit is not usually readily available from the accounting records. Audits, therefore, include estimates and judgments. If the audit were performed by a group with an interest in the project, they would be tempted to justify the original analysis. It should be noted, however, that no matter where audit responsibility is placed, because of the lack of objective data, there will be some chance of bias. The best approach is to structure the performance of audits to reduce bias to a minimum.

Regardless of where the audit responsibility is placed, the division which originated the financial analysis must participate in the audit. This involvement cannot be underemphasized. Each manager should have his eye on the profitability of the total organization. By his decisions, profitability is assured or diluted. Therefore, to have a division submit a project and then not participate in the original financial analysis of the project or in the presentation of the actual results is to fail to make maximum use of the resources available for an accurate evaluation and a failure to identify the best decisions which lead to maximum profits. If the originating department is involved in the audit, it can learn from the errors made and re-examine its estimating and evaluation and control procedures. In addition, by participating in the audit, the originating organization can collect and summarize the final results by the individuals who submitted the original proposals. Corrective action could require a change in methodology, in record keeping, in personnel, or it could mean a change in the objectives sought. However, whatever change is required, for the full benefits from analyses to be realized, the submitting organization must be involved! The best procedure to assure participation is to document each analysis as thoroughly as possible and require the originating group to present both the original analysis and the audit to top management for approval and review.

The Functions of the Auditor

The financial division should, after approval, assign a number to the project, and hold a copy for audit. If the life of an analysis were five years, it would not be necessary to wait five years for an audit. An interim audit could be made after a few months or after one or two years to check the progress of the project. However, the auditors must measure the interim report results by methodology similar to that which was used for the financial analysis. By having the originating group and the financial organization participate in the review and approval of both the analysis and the audit, increased coordination of the organization's work is encouraged. The originator becomes involved with the results of his decision. In this way, the audit group acts as an integrator as well as a guardian of cost control.

Auditing Techniques

Generally, the techniques used for preparing financial analyses and the subsequent audits are standard discounted cash flow programs available in most computers. These programs compare cash outflows and inflows to determine the rate at which, discounted to present value, they are equal. For estimating, the best techniques are simple linear regression or multiple linear regression analyses. In some cases, when evaluating marketing programs, it may be best to use the technique of pro forma statements in order to determine the effect of alternative marketing programs upon fixed costs. Similar statements should be prepared for the post audit to facilitate comparability and accurate evaluation of the original analysis.

Summary

To summarize, the basic approach to the preparation and audit of financial analyses is cut and try. Experience results in refining the estimating techniques and the methods for gathering data. Cost control depends upon the accuracy of the estimates. If the amounts spent are equal to or less than the estimates, cost control has been achieved.

As learning from results occurs, more accurate analyses and projections are possible. It should be remembered that even though better techniques might be available at the time of post audit, the originator of the project did not necessarily have these techniques available to him. This is important to note because the time which has elapsed between initiation and completion of a project can influence the evaluation. For example, if simple linear regression analysis was used in the original analysis, but it has become apparent that at the time of audit a multiple linear regression formula will produce better results, it should be at least noted that at the time the original analysis was prepared the importance of the additional variables was not known. In almost every case, financial analysis and the subsequent audit will be facilitated if the computations can be made on data processing equipment. However, there are techniques available which can be used manually as was illustrated in Chapter 2.

Chapter 4

Forecast Reporting for Increased Profits

FORECASTING AND PLANNING ARE TWO DISTINCT PROCEDURES. Planning is a more formal process which requires a definition of objectives and the strategies by which the objectives are to be accomplished. To these objectives and strategies, a financial plan is added. Plans provide a target for the whole organization and all parts of the organization participate in the planning process. Plans are generally more forward looking or cover a longer period of time than a forecast. A typical planning cycle is for the budget year (the next fiscal year) plus four additional years into the future. Forecasting, on the other hand, is short-range. As circumstances change after the budget year has begun, these changes are recognized in the forecast. Forecasting begins at the end of the first month of the budget year. At this time, a forecast is prepared which includes the actual results for the first month and a forecast for the remainder of the period.

Forecasting Increases Profits

Usually, by the beginning of the fiscal year, the budget has been completed and is the organization's financial objective. However, with the exception of the most stable environments, by the time the fiscal year begins, the organization's circumstances have changed, such as demand for its product, or changes in costs of materials, and labor at rates other than those anticipated in the budget. The methods and processes for manufacturing a product have probably been altered because of unexpected shortages of materials and unanticipated technological innovations. At the beginning of the fiscal year, operating conditions are more fully defined and the economic as well as marketing circumstances for the coming year are more easily interpreted. Forecasting for the fiscal year provides the organization with a direction which is more congruent with its current situation and improves decisions.

The forecast, when compared to the actual results, will indicate where results and the forecast are deviating. Each comparison must include the variation from the forecast. The variances identified are the basis for at least two typical reactions: (a) corrective action to change the results achieved; or (b) the forecast is revised to more closely match the results!

To keep the firm on a profitable path and before any action can be taken, the variances from the forecast must be identified. After identification, the variances need to be investigated to determine whether the forecast was inaccurate or whether the plan was not followed by operating managers! Investigation of the variances will cause both a revision of the forecast and corrective action to bring the actual results more in line with the forecast. Reactions to the variances from forecast are not predictable and could range from a reduction or delay in incurring costs to the separation of personnel. However, variance analysis will result in better decisions. And better decisions maximize profits especially in an adverse economic environment.

If losses are not anticipated, they cannot be avoided. One manufacturer, for example, prepares plans six months in advance and rarely revises them. This organization has too short-range an approach and thereby limits its ability to react to change. For example, if this firm needed to reduce costs, the plan would not forewarn management. If management were aware of the problem earlier, such as at the end of the first month of the fiscal year, they could react and make the appropriate changes. When the need to reduce costs by $10,000 is not recognized until six months of the fiscal year have passed, the result may be the termination of two people instead of one. The sooner forecasting begins, the better the adjustment of the whole organization.

The Certainty of Change

Rapid change is an important and perpetual part of the business environment. Plans which were developed six, four or even three months before they are implemented may be completely or partially obsolete. To compensate for this possibility, the organization should not continually replan — that involves too extensive an investment in resources — but must be prepared to modify plans, daily if necessary, through a less formal procedure.

Imagine an organization which has expended large quantities of time and effort on an operating plan. However, before the plan has been executed, the market has changed because consumers have changed their buying habits. Raw material, required in the manufacturing process, is no longer available. It is irrational for an organization to assume, regardless of the planning effort expended, that the circumstances that were anticipated for the plan will duplicate reality. They can at best approximate it. The organization must be prepared to abandon even the most costly plan.

Today, in many organizations, it is unusual to find long-service employees. Employees are more mobile, their expectations change, their values are influenced each day. The business firm's relationships with the government and its agencies change very rapidly. New laws, restrictions, governmental objectives and taxes are introduced continually. Business is change.

Organizations have a choice. They can anticipate change and take advantage of the opportunities changes can produce or they can wait and react defensively. A good example was the fuel crisis.

> One manufacturer which markets both electric and gasoline driven tools saw an opportunity when the fuel crisis arose. They switched their emphasis from gasoline tools to similar electric tools which could perform the same functions. This change required a re-examination of their advertising and an evaluation of their inventory to see if there were enough electric tools in stock to justify the additional expenditures

on advertising. It also meant they had to check their methods of distribution. Distributors sometimes specialize in the types of tools which they sell best. The manufacturer had to be certain he was prepared for those distributors who had the ability to sell electric tools. Additionally, prices had to be re-examined to be certain they were right for the change in marketing thrust. They turned a crisis to their advantage!

Forecasting Prepares the Firm for Short-Run Change

It is best to reforecast at the end of the first month of the fiscal year and to update that forecast each month. One large manufacturer of aircraft has found changes and adjustments in its research program so rapid that costs of each program are gathered weekly. Each week every research program is reforecast for the current fiscal year and, in some cases, beyond. Another very successful manufacturer develops a five-year plan. The plan consists of a yearly estimate for four years and the budget for the next fiscal year. At the end of each month after the budget period begins, each division of the organization reforecasts the fiscal year. They are rarely surprised when changes occur and adjustments are necessary.

Forecasting Is Used for the Analysis of Organization Strengths and Weaknesses

All organizations must measure their strengths and weaknesses against the requirements of the market. As the market changes, the organization must adjust to the change and become more attuned to the demands of its market. For example, the organization must be prepared to re-examine its research efforts. Usually, research can be classified as basic or developmental. The developmental phase involves relatively short time periods and the basic phase includes relatively long-range projects. By re-examining the sales forecasts each month, the needs of the market are recognized and the research effort adjusted to avoid wasting this resource on the wrong products. When forecasting, the inventory budgets must be investigated to determine whether the correct quantities of the correct products are being accumulated. It is almost certain that those who did not forecast during the energy crisis were caught with the wrong products in inventory for the existing market. The inventory levels of big cars at that time was a very costly error for the United States auto industry.

To identify organizational strengths and weaknesses and take advantage of strengths some important questions must be answered:

1. Are prices and discounts correct for this fiscal year? The auto industry is again an illustration of a lack of forecasting. Had they been continually reforecasting market conditions, they would have discounted the bigger cars and firmed up the prices of the smaller models.
2. Is staffing balanced to the market? The energy crisis created an environment where it would have been best to emphasize product improvement and more money should have been spent on research to make the product perform the same function more efficiently. To do this it is necessary to have enough trained engineers to effect product redesigns.
3. Are the right costs recognized? If energy costs increase, it might be possible to redesign the product to reduce operating costs.

A practical example of adjusting through forecasting is that of a manufacturer of small tools.

> At the end of each month, sales are reforecast by tool, using the A,B,C, principle which is 80 percent of the anticipated volume will be in a few (approximately 20-30 percent) popular tools. This procedure is continued until approximately 80 percent of the volume has been reforecast. This reduces the cost and time spent reforecasting. Advertising can then be adjusted to support those tools which the reforecast indicated are not selling as they should. From the reforecast, manufacturing schedules can be adjusted to support the inventory level which is indicated. With this technique, the manufacturer did an excellent job of adjusting to the changes in his market. His profit increased as others' profits decreased or remained stable. Thus, continual adjustment increased profits. Profits accrue from using organization strengths, not weaknesses.

How to Forecast

The first step is to reproject sales by major products for each remaining month of the fiscal year. These forecasts can be made by the sales force or based upon the best judgment of the in-house marketing executives. In addition, historical ratios can be used to project the future, or the applicable parts of a rolling forecast can be added to the actual costs to compute fiscal year totals. (A rolling forecast is a twelve-month forecast which is adjusted as each month's actual is computed. The month for which the actual is available is dropped and another month is added as the twelfth month). It should be noted that it is possible to use a combination of these methods as well as use one method to check the accuracy of another.

Based upon the revised sales forecast, cost of sales must be recalculated. Cost of sales can be recomputed either by using current standard product costs for major products multiplied by the estimated quantities to be sold, plus an historically based projection for the remainder of the products or it can be calculated by using projected sales to cost of sales ratios. If ratios are used, recent history as well as a rolling forecast can be the data base for reprojecting the fiscal year. The ratio forecast can be adjusted easily for modifications in historical ratios which the corporate executives might think necessary; simply add or subtract their input from the results.

Additionally, expenses must be reprojected. Selling expenses should correlate with the latest sales estimate. If selling expenses are largely salesmen's commissions, it will be easy to adjust to the new sales level. If, however, salaried salesmen are employed, then the percentage of selling expense will increase as sales decrease and vice versa. Also, the addition of salesmen or changes in travel allowances or other expenses must be anticipated. Usually, with selling expenses, judgment based upon current history with adjustment for any foreseen marketing changes is the best method for reforecasting. Next, administrative expenses must be reprojected. This again must be a judgment estimate using recent history and any knowledge of changes that might take place within the fiscal year.

After the forecast is completed, the computed net income is evaluated by comparing it to the organizational objectives. If the forecast net income is lower than that sought by management, a plan should be prepared to alter the forecast so it meets the objectives sought. This could cause expense reductions, or a formal cost reduction program to be initiated such as a reduction of purchases, delaying of purchases or the layoff or separation of personnel. The action needed might be the redirection of the sales effort. An example of modifying the sales effort is to promote products which are already in inventory or products with short manufacturing cycles. To do this, incremental pricing is an alternative with which to get additional sales by only covering the variable expenses including a contribution towards fixed costs.

There are a number of techniques that have varying levels of sophistication, by which forecasts can be prepared. Three widely used methods are: econometric models, naive projections or judgmental estimates.

Econometric Models. To develop an econometric model, study and/or research are required to identify a model of the economy which managers of the firm consider reliable for their purposes. The model chosen must relate to the particular industry in which the firm operates. The purpose is to identify a variable or a set of variables which are both included in the model and are a determinant of industry sales. Once this has been accomplished, the firm can relate its sales to the industry of which it is a part. The most effective method for relating the firm to an industry is through computing the firm's market share. Once industry sales have been projected from the econometric model, then the estimated percentage of the firm's market share can be used to predict the firm's sales. From this total, cost of sales and expenses can be deducted to arrive at forecast net income.

Naive Projections. A naive projection is the projecting of the recent past into the future. This method can be used to forecast sales, cost of sales, expenses, and net income. This technique is based upon the assumption that current events will continue into the future. It is usually a straight-line projection of the past.

Judgmental Estimates. Another alternative is the use of judgment. The judgment of corporate managers and knowledgeable members of the organization is often as good an estimate as is possible. For sales, the forecast would be prepared by in-house marketing executives or by the supervisors of the field sales force. For expenses, administrators responsible for each group and for each expense category should prepare the forecast. In each case, they estimate by judgment and project that into the future. Forecasts can also be prepared from combinations of these methods.

Examples of Forecasting Techniques

Exhibit 8 is an example of a naive projection of historical trends for a small manufacturer. Because this method is inexpensive and relatively accurate, the naive trend is effective for this application. This manufacturer needed to forecast his sales in order to plan inventory levels. While too much inventory is costly, too little inventory can result in lost sales. By formalizing his plans and looking at them in a reasonable way, he was able to correlate his material, cash and personnel needs. This manufacturer could foresee change, make the necessary adjustments and profitably take advantage of the future. By the use of the forecast, this manufacturer was able to maximize his sales, cut costs and increase his profits by 10%.

Exhibit 9 is an example of a judgment forecast for a softgoods manufacturer. One difficulty with this method is that it relies upon the experience of the forecaster for accuracy and validity. It is dependent upon the knowledge of the individual. If continuity of personnel is enforced within the organization, this may not be a serious problem. However, to rely on the individual instead of the organizational system may mean that the ability of the firm to forecast is dependent upon one person or a small group. The main objective is to document the judgment forecasts. While the forecast is dependent upon human judgment, formalizing the forecast will record the assumptions upon which it was based and facilitate adjustments. While this is the least structured of the forecasting techniques it is superior to spontaneous planning and the resultant poor decisions.

The softgoods manufacturer illustrated here is a medium size, privately held firm. The experience of the company executives is still the guide line used for planning, but better control and more careful scrutiny of the underlying assumptions have resulted not only in more accurate and meaningful forecasts for this firm, but also greater profits.

Exhibit 10 is an example of an econometric model used for forecasting for a large clothing manufacturer. First the manufacturer chose a model of the economy upon which to base his forecast. Then he related the industry to a variable included in the economic model. Then the firm related its share of market to the estimated sales for the industry. From this, the firm's sales forecast was prepared. Also, this forecast was checked by preparation of a judgment estimate. It is desirable, if the resources are available, to check a forecast by using more than one technique.

By the use of an econometric model, a firm can gain more accurate knowledge of its market and market position. The study and expertise used to build the model is also a useful data bank from which a firm can learn more about its environment. Modeling results in a more reliable and useful forecast than any other method. However, because this method is expensive, it is only appropriate when the resources are available and the organization's environment is complex.

The large clothing manufacturer whose forecast is illustrated in Exhibit 10 was able to use the predictions in the model to determine the potential market and gear its production to the largest segment. Continued use of the model will allow them to adjust their products to this rapidly changing market. While other firms failed because of their inability to satisfy changing consumer tastes, this firm was able to maintain its share of market and its profitability.

Summary

Forecasting is necessary to anticipate change. It is more applicable to the business entity in the short run, i.e., the current fiscal year. It is extremely important that the firm continually readjust to meet the future. The firm cannot wait until the future is upon it. The necessary adjustments cannot happen unless the firm looks to the future. This is the peculiar advantage of forecasting. To forecast, each firm can choose the methodology most compatible with its resources. There are a number of methods from which to choose and the firm can choose the one which best suits its needs for the time and money it wishes to invest in a forecasting technique.

EXHIBIT 8

NAIVE FORECAST OF HISTORICAL TRENDS
SMALL CLOTHING MANUFACTURER

Month and Year		Net Sales	Cost of Goods Sold	Gross Margin	Expenses	Profit Before Inc. Taxes
Actual						
Month	1	$ 60,000	$ 48,000	$12,000	$ 7,500	$ 4,500
	2	48,000	40,800	7,200	4,300	2,900
	3	39,200	33,320	5,880	4,480	1,400
	4	26,700	22,700	4,000	5,000	(1,000)
	5	43,000	36,600	6,400	4,400	2,000
	6	55,400	46,000	9,400	6,200	3,200
	7	39,700	33,700	6,000	4,900	1,100
	8	36,000	30,600	5,400	4,400	1,000
	9	44,900	38,200	6,700	4,800	1,900
	10	19,700	16,700	3,000	5,000	(2,000)
	11	48,000	40,800	7,200	4,200	3,000
	12	41,300	35,100	6,200	4,100	2,100
Total FY	1	$501,900	$422,520	$79,380	$59,280	$20,100
Forecast						
Month	1 (Actual)	$ 72,000	$ 58,300	$13,700	$ 7,900	$ 5,800
	2 (Actual)	54,000	45,400	8,600	4,800	3,800
	3	45,700	38,400	7,300	5,300	2,000
	4	31,200	26,200	5,000	4,400	600
	5	50,200	42,200	8,000	5,500	2,500
	6	64,700	54,300	10,400	6,400	4,000
	7	46,300	38,900	7,400	5,300	2,100
	8	42,000	35,300	6,700	5,000	1,700
	9	52,400	44,000	8,400	5,600	2,800
	10	23,000	19,300	3,700	3,900	(200)
	11	56,000	47,000	9,000	5,800	3,200
	12	48,200	40,500	7,700	5,400	2,300
Total FY	2	$585,700	$489,800	$95,900	$65,300	$30,600

NOTES:

1. This projection could be done on a graph instead of in columnar form.
2. The sales forecast is a projection of the average sales increase for the first two months (16.7%).
3. Cost of Goods Sold is projected on the basis of last year's percent (84.0%)

4. Expenses are projected as $30,000 of Fixed Expenses increased by 3% plus 5.8% of monthly sales which is the same percent of sales for Variable Expenses as the percent of total variable expenses to sales for the last fiscal year.

EXHIBIT 9

JUDGMENT FORECAST FOR A SOFTGOODS MANUFACTURER

(000)

Month and Year	Net Sales	Cost of Sales	Gross Profit	Variable General Expenses	Fixed General Expenses	Net Income Before Inc. Taxes
Actual						
Month 1	$ 17,000	$ 11,900	$ 5,100	$ 1,000	$ 2,200	$ 1,900
2	15,800	11,900	3,900	800	2,400	700
3	14,900	11,000	3,900	600	2,000	1,300
4	13,700	10,900	2,800	500	2,100	200
5	15,300	11,300	4,000	700	2,300	1,000
6	16,500	11,300	5,200	1,000	2,300	1,900
7	15,000	12,000	3,000	700	2,000	300
8	14,600	11,200	3,400	600	2,100	700
9	15,500	12,100	3,400	800	2,200	400
10	13,000	10,400	2,600	500	2,400	(300)
11	15,800	11,700	4,100	900	2,000	1,200
12	15,100	11,800	3,300	700	2,500	100
Total FY	$182,200	$137,500	$44,700	$ 8,800	$26,500	$ 9,400
Month 1	$ 17,500	$ 12,300	$ 5,200	$ 1,200	$ 2,300	$ 1,700
2	16,000	11,700	4,300	1,000	2,500	800
Forecast 3	15,600	12,200	3,400	800	2,400	200
Month 4	15,600	12,000	3,600	800	2,200	600
5	16,000	11,500	4,500	900	2,200	1,400
6	17,200	12,100	5,100	1,100	2,200	1,800
7	16,500	11,300	5,200	1,000	2,200	2,000
8	16,000	11,500	4,500	900	2,200	1,400
9	16,000	11,500	4,500	900	2,200	1,400
10	15,700	12,000	3,700	800	2,200	700
11	16,200	11,400	4,800	900	2,200	1,700
12	16,300	11,400	4,900	900	2,400	1,600
Total FY	$194,600	$140,900	$53,700	$11,200	$27,200	$15,300

NOTES:

1. The Forecast Sales were estimated by major products by the Central Marketing Staff.
2. The Forecast Cost of Sales was computed by multiplying the estimated units to be sold of high volume items by their standard cost plus a variation percent. A percentage relationship between Sales and Cost of Sales was used for the remainder (low volume) items.
3. General Expenses were estimated by each department supervisor whose department is included in this category. These estimates were then totaled by Fixed and Variable components to arrive at the monthly forecast.

EXHIBIT 10

ECONOMETRIC FORECASTING MODEL

(000)

1. This model was selected as most representative of the United States economy. It is a rough simulation of a more highly sophisticated model used by government and some business consultants.
2. The assumptions underlying this model are listed below:

a. Unemployment Rate	5.7%
b. Inflation Rate	5.0%
c. Increase In The Money Supply	9.0%
d. Investment Tax Credit	7.0%
e. The Industrial Production Index	111.3%
f. Average Propensity To Save	7.5%

3. The model was used to prepare a five-year financial plan. During the second month of the first year of that plan, the model was rerun to compute a reforecast of the current year and a new five-year plan.
4. Model In Total (Mil.) (Current Dollars)

Year	Gross Product National	Consumption	Investment	Government Spending	Net Exports
1	$1,128,200.0	$715,000.0	$163,100.0	$248,300.0	$1,800.0
2	1,182,200.0	756,900.0	164,000.0	258,900.0	2,400.0
3	1,234,200.0	801,200.0	167,900.0	262,900.0	2,200.0
4	1,298,800.0	848,300.0	174,300.0	274,200.0	2,000.0
5	1,366,500.0	898,500.0	180,700.0	285,500.0	1,800.0
6	1,437,500.0	952,000.0	187,100.0	296,800.0	1,600.0

5. Disaggregation of Consumption Expenditures:

Year	Total Consumption Expenditures	(Mil.) Durable Goods	(Current Dollars) Non-Durable Goods	Services
1	$715,000.0	$108,900.0	$296,000.0	$303,500.0
2	756,900.0	116,700.0	311,400.0	328,800.0
3	801,200.0	119,200.0	327,600.0	354,400.0
4	848,300.0	121,700.9	344,600.0	382,000.0
5	898,500.9	124,200.0	362,500.0	411,800.0
6	952,000.0	126,700.0	381,400.0	443,900.0

6. Disaggregation of Non-Durable Goods Expenditures For Forecast Year:

(000) (Current Dollars)

Year	Total Non Durable Goods	Total Soft Goods X	Other
1	296,000,000.0	589,000,000.0	237,100,000.0

This calculation is based upon a correlation analysis of 24 years data including the year prior to the current year. The variables included in the analysis are Expenditures on Non-Durable Goods, Population (Millions) and the Consumer Price Ratio which were regressed upon expenditures for Soft Goods X.

7. Total Estimated Sales of Soft Goods X is then related to Sales of Soft Goods X+1.

(000) (Current Dollars)

Year	Total Soft Goods X	Total Soft Goods X+1	Other
1	58,909,000.0	4,036,000.0	54,864,000.0

The calculation for Soft Good X+1 includes a 24-year period and included are additional variables such as the Male Population Age 25-65 in millions and the Wholesale Price Index Price Ratio.

8. The estimated sales of the firm are related to the projected sales of Soft Good X+1.

(000) (Current Dolars)

Year	Sales of Soft Good X+1	Firm Sales	Other
1	4,036,000.0	58,700.0	3,977,300.0

This calculation included eleven years data and additional variables.

9. Finally, the latest sales forecast must be disaggregated and the cost factors applied.

(000) (Current Dollars)

Months	Sales	Cost of Sales	Gross Margin	General Expenses	Income Before Income Taxes
Actual					
1	$ 7,009.4	$ 5,607.5	$ 1,401.9	$ 972.8	$ 429.1
2	5,614.8	4,660.3	954.5	766.4	188.1
Forecast					
3	4,580.6	3,733.0	847.6	700.0	147.6
4	3,122.7	2,545.9	577.7	600.0	(22.3)
5	5,035.7	4,104.0	931.7	744.0	187.7
6	6,480.6	5,282.0	1,198.6	910.0	288.6
7	4,642.6	3,784.0	858.6	705.0	153.6
8	4,216.7	3,436.0	780.7	711.0	69.7
9	5,252.1	4,280.0	972.1	750.6	222.1
10	2,303.7	1,878.0	425.7	550.0	(124.3)
11	5,611.3	4,573.0	1,038.3	900.0	138.3
12	4,829.8	3,936.0	893.8	700.0	193.8
Total	$58,700.0	$47,818.8	$10,881.2	$9,009.2	$1,872.0

The cost factors are based upon a time series analysis of eleven years history, including the year prior to the current or forecast year.

EXHIBIT 11

This exhibit illustrates the importance of variance analysis and is based upon the disaggregation of the fixed expense included in Exhibit 9. The fixed expenses included in forecast month 4 of Exhibit 9 are equal to $2,200,000. For this illustration it is assumed that the detail of those expenses is:

Account Description	Amount
Accounting Department Expense	$ 200,000
Purchasing Department Expense	300,000
Personnel Department Expense	400,000
Legal Department Expenses	150,000
Executive Department Expenses	150,000
Liability Insurance Expense	500,000
Rent Expense	300,000
Supplies Expense	200,000
Total	$2,200,000

These forecast amounts are compared to the actual results by each account to identify variances. As an example, the following variance report was prepared:

Account Description	Actual Amount	Budget Amount	Variance ( ) = Unfavorable
Accounting Department Expense	$ 300,000	$ 200,000	($100,000)
Purchasing Department Expense	250,000	300,000	50,000
Personnel Department Expense	600,000	400,000	(200,000)
Legal Department Expense	200,000	150,000	(50,000)
Executive Department Expense	200,000	150,000	(50,000)
Liability Insurance Expense	700,000	500,000	(200,000)
Rent Expense	350,000	300,000	(50,000)
Supplies Expense	100,000	200,000	100,000
Total	$2,700,000	$2,200,000	($500,000)

Each variance should be investigated to determine the cause. Depending upon the causes identified, the investigation of variances can lead to a review of the strategy, the operating policy, the cost structure and the prices for the entire firm.

If the analysis of the variances does not indicate a significant deviation from the original objectives, the forecast will be adjusted to the new level of activity.

The following examples illustrate the causes such an analysis usually identifies: (a) The Accounting Department Expense — the $100,000 unfavorable variance from the forecast was caused by a failure to anticipate all expenses. Therefore, the forecast must be adjusted. Assuming the variance is significant to the firm, either a price increase is necessary or a reduction in personnel must be initiated to offset the unforeseen expenses; (b) The excess Personnel Department Expenses of $200,000 were caused by the unexpected need to recruit additional personnel. (Variances of $50,000 or less are considered insignificant and therefore, not included in this analysis.) A number of unplanned resignations of executive personnel caused the initiation of an active recruitment program. Because this program is apparently a one-time expense, no revision to the forecast of personnel department expenses is necessary. However, an attempt will be made to increase the sales forecast to recover the amount spent for recruiting. (c) The Liability Insurance Expense—the $200,000 unfavorable variance was caused by a rate adjustment because of an increase in the number of claims filed against the firm. Investigation of the variance indicates that it cannot be recovered through increased sales, consequently, the forecast net income for the firm was reduced by the amount of increase in the liability insurance premium; and (d) The Supplies Expense was $100,000 less than expected. Because no reasonable explanation for the decrease in the supplies expense was identified, the forecast is not revised. Assuming that supplies expense may be larger than anticipated in the future, or that other expenses may have been underestimated, the amount not spent on supplies will be kept in reserve to cover these contingencies.

The report illustrated is a cumulative report for a six-month period. However, variance analysis reports can be prepared weekly, monthly, quarterly and cumulatively for the same periods. Actual results for direct materials and direct labor are usually available weekly, for other expenses only monthly information is usually available. Regardless of when the actual information is available, the variance analysis report is a flexible report and it can be tailored to fit any time period.

Chapter 5

Using Incremental Cost Analysis to Maintain and Improve Efficiency

INCREMENTAL COSTING IS THE ANALYSIS OF THE EFFECT UPON COSTS of a change in the operating methods or procedures of a business organization. It identifies the costs that change with a change in operations. It is the evaluation of alternatives based upon an analysis of only those costs which are affected by the choices.

Incremental Costing Keeps the Firm Abreast of Changing Business Climates

Incremental costing is a useful tool for taking advantage of the firm's fixed investment and for helping an organization through economic adversity. As a method for the solution of problems, incremental costing can be used to minimize losses by emphasizing the importance of out-of-pocket costs rather than full costs. Business literature is full of examples of poor decisions that were made based on full costs which included complete allocations of overhead, fixed, and discretionary costs.

Full cost analysis is important, and to be successful an organization must recover its full costs and make a profit. However, there are circumstances when incremental costing is applicable and can help an organization reach the objective of maximum profit. This technique emphasizes the identification of sunk costs that are not relevant to a particular decision. An analysis of a firm's cost structure is required to identify those costs which are variable and those which are fixed for the purpose of the particular decision to be made.

Incremental costing minimizes the importance of sunk costs when making short-run decisions, particularly those decisions which involve survival of the firm during a recession or depression. As a corollary, incremental costing suggests the use of incremental pricing when demand is decreasing. By determining the incremental costs of a product, the firm is in a position to price on an incremental rather than a full cost basis. If the product can be priced so that variable costs are recovered and there is a remaining contribution to fixed costs, the firm will be better off than it would be if it didn't operate at all. Although resources must be consumed to identify which costs are fixed and which are variable, the benefits from such an analysis, i.e., the knowledge to incrementally price, outweigh the short-run costs. One difficulty caused by incremental pricing is the possibility of spoiling the market. However, when the issue is survival of the firm, it is better to spoil the market (which may be temporary) than destroy the firm.

There will, however, be many instances when the answer is not this clear. The firm will survive, but perhaps not at the growth rate nor in its current form and size. Therefore, the decision may be to maintain market price and reduce the scale of operations. The determining factors in such a case are the extent and length of the recessionary period as well as the changes in, and nature of, the market demand for the firm's products.

Incremental Costing Emphasizes the Use of Internal Leverage to Increase Profits

Incremental costing is a particularly beneficial analytical tool for determining the causes of the overall profitability of a firm. One advantage of this method is trading on internal leverage to increase profits. When the question is whether to introduce a new product or discontinue an old one, the decision must be based on only those costs that are affected by the change. During periods of excess capacity, it will often be more profitable to introduce a new product, although price covers only variable costs and makes a contribution to fixed costs, than not to introduce a product at all. Again, however, this is dependent upon the alternatives available, including the risk of success or failure of the new product in the market. When considering eliminating a product it must be remembered that the overhead associated with the discontinued product will have to be absorbed elsewhere because overhead does not disappear when a product is dropped. The most important advantage of incremental costing is that it forces the evaluation of alternative uses of economic resources based upon only pertinent costs.

Incremental Costing Can Help Increase Productivity and Efficiency

Usually, incremental costing is related to product introduction, discontinuance or replacement decisions. However, this is only one application. The failure to apply incremental costing to other decisions results in reduced profits.

For example, the replacement of manual operations with automatic data processing on an existing computer is a decision that should be based upon the costs that change, but not the costs of the computer itself. The cost of the existing computer is sunk and not relevant to the decision. The addition of a salesman or a new territory involves consideration of costs directly related to the salesman. The supervisors of the sales force will be there regardless. The point is that in any case where a relatively fixed cost is involved, the financial evaluation should be made ignoring that cost. It is usually argued that this approach will eventually lead to an increased investment in fixed costs. This is not necessarily true. By treating fixed costs as discretionary in nature, a decision for their regression or expansion is a prerogative of management to be made under the particular circumstances at the time.

In the case of the computer, for example, the argument is often presented that there is a limit to the number of hours of time available. However, investigation indicates that the more pressure put on the data processing organization to use the computer efficiently the more efficiently it is used! Usually they will find better and more efficient ways of using the computer such as not using it as a sorter, etc. This technique is also applicable in the case of sales supervision where often the sales manager finds more efficient means of supervising and therefore expansion of the supervisory staff is not required.

The Human Organization Can Be Maintained Through Incremental Costing

Another important advantage of incremental costing is that under adverse economic conditions the use of this technique can result in the maintenance of the human organization despite a poor economy. Generally, when business firms face adverse economic conditions, they react either by reducing their price in response to decreased demand or by maintaining their price and reducing the level of operations. It should be noted that there are also numerous combinations of these reactions depending upon the number of markets served and whether the markets are reasonably competitive, oligopolistic or monopolistic.

By adjusting the firm's price and basing it upon incremental costs with some contribution to fixed costs, the human organization can be maintained. If the emphasis is placed upon those costs that vary with a change in operations, decreases in the level of sales do not necessarily mean employees will be separated from the organization. Concentration on full costs can result in the failure to maintain the human organization that might be needed during a period of economic recovery. Because there may be a level of operations where most costs, including fixed or discretionary costs, do change, requiring for example that a foreman be hired or fired, the relevant operating range must be kept in mind. Therefore, incremental costing must be evaluated in terms of the relevant range of activity within which discretionary costs remain relatively stable. The principle of incremental costing is still valid if the level of production activity exceeds or drops below the relevant range, but the effect upon discretionary costs must be more closely evaluated under these circumstances. In the long run, it may be better to incrementally cost and price and keep the employees you will need when production activity increases.

The benefit of this course is priceless: Keeping the firm's staff employed in an adverse economy can cause feelings of satisfaction and generate loyalty among employees that will pay off in both immediate and future profits.

Incremental Pricing and Market Share

There is also a cost to taking and maintaining market share. The firm should analyze in depth, the benefits from continuing operations by incremental pricing versus surrendering market share. When this alternative is compared to the costs of recapturing market share, the results of the analysis may indicate it is more profitable to reduce prices and maintain or possibly improve market position.

The Learning Curve and Incremental Costing

Incremental costing is useful for evaluating the firm's cost structure. Costs and levels of activity are seldom related, but to be profitable a firm must understand its cost structure. Costs and production activity must be closely correlated to determine which costs change with changes in production activity. This requires intensive study to determine to what extent costs change and to identify unusual blips as well as irrelevant changes in both sets of data. Production activity is generally considered to be the most important determinant of changes in costs, but this is only part of the function of incremental costing. Costs that change with fluctuations in sales activity can also be identified through incremental analysis. Important decisions require identification of traceable, direct, and variable costs, thereby permitting a logical evaluation of the possible results of such a decision.

Additionally an in-depth analysis of costs will identify weaknesses in the accounting records. Accounting records maintained for tax and reporting purposes, are based upon the principle of full costing. This means fixed and variable expense components are not separated and classified as such, and the fixed and variable portion of any particular expense is not segregated and identified.

The objectives of the analysis should be to identify incremental costs for which the traditional accounting approach is not adequate. As a result of this search, the accounting records may be modified or alternative approaches devised for measuring the variable and fixed costs and possibly the maintenance of a separate set of analytical records apart from the accounting records. This does not necessarily mean duplication. It could be a set of formulas which can be applied to the accounting records to derive the information needed for incremental analysis. If it accomplishes nothing else, the analysis of a firm's costs for the purpose of incremental costing trains personnel how to use incremental costing for making decisions and to organize and collect data with incremental analysis as the objective. In this way, employees become familiar with the use of a very important analytical technique as well as gain experience in gathering data pertinent to the decision-making process.

At the least, incremental analysis will provide data for computing the contribution of each particular product. The contribution margin is defined as the net sales of the product less the product variable costs. Product variable costs include not only the direct costs traceable to that product, but all costs that vary with the production of that product, or costs that change with a change in the output of a product. This includes more than the employees working directly on the product such as machinists; it includes those employees who supply parts or record the time worked by direct employees. Even though the cost of an indirect worker may not be totally absorbed by a product, without that product it may mean the employee works less hours and therefore costs less to the firm. It must be emphasized, therefore, that contribution margin includes variable indirect costs related to a product as well as costs directly associated and traceable to that product.

Marketing Contribution Margin

As with product costs, it is necessary that a contribution margin for each market be computed. The market is generally defined as a sales territory, although it could be further defined as an area covered by each salesman if sales territories include more than one man. It is vital for an organization to know the contribution of each of its sales markets. This is a simple computation which involves capturing net sales by territory and deducting the variable costs of the product sold in that market plus the variable selling expenses such as salesman's salaries, travel expenses, costs for credit administration, and the costs of returns and allowances. The result of deducting these costs is the incremental contribution of each market.

Through this technique, a number of rankings of profitability can be developed, such as products within each market or ranges of markets, from the most profitable to the least profitable. It should be realized that ranking requires continual re-evaluation because of the dynamism of change caused by implementation of cost reduction programs, market changes, products being added, dropped, and substituted. There is a high probability that rankings will change continuously, therefore, they must be continually updated.

How to Use Incremental Costing to Gain Market Share

Incremental costing is very useful for reviewing and evaluating pricing policy. Incremental pricing, which results from incremental costing, is a useful tool for gaining market share through lower prices. The objective is, in good times, to take market share from competitors and, in bad times, to maintain market share. The effect of a price reduction, from incremental costing, is increased volume and increased profits through spreading fixed costs over more production. However, it must be emphasized that pricing policy is influenced by demand for the product. Therefore, pricing must be compatible with demand, i.e., prices cannot be lowered to the point that demand will outstrip the organization's ability to produce, or when lower prices will not increase volume. In this sense, it would be foolish to expand facilities without recovering full costs. This decision, however, must be carefully evaluated because the volume increase from lower prices on a number of products may more than adequately cover fixed costs and contribute to profits. This process is highly dynamic and continual evaluation will result in adjustment of the product mix.

For example, products which cannot benefit from incremental pricing may be dropped and emphasis placed upon products with which market share can be captured. In addition, at low volumes a drop in the price of some products will not result in a volume increase to contribute sufficiently to fixed costs. But a slight drop in the price of a complementary product may more than offset that lack of response. The firm, by adjusting its product mix based upon the results of incremental analysis, will be able to withstand changes in the economy and maintain stability. Competitors who full-cost price will provide an umbrella under which firms that incremental-price can take share of market and more than justify the incremental approach. However, the effect of incremental pricing upon the sales force must not be overlooked. It is possible that a product which is to be discontinued is the product that is most easily sold or which the sales force is best trained to sell. In this case, the salesmen should be retrained or the product kept in the line as other products are slowly introduced and the sales emphasis shifted. In any case, without incremental costing, there cannot be incremental pricing.

Taking Advantage of Fixed Costs

Incremental costing could be called "trading upon internal fixed costs." Fixed costs are ignored in short-run decisions. In addition to being irrelevant to short-run decisions, generally, the larger the output which includes some contribution to fixed costs, the greater will be the profit. As output increases, the firm learns more about its products and processes and there is movement down the learning curve which will cause the organization's total costs to decrease as output increases. Learning will also contribute to development of more efficient marketing techniques and increasing volume, because of the effect upon learning, will increase the contribution to fixed costs as well as contribute to a substantial profit.

As was pointed out in Chapter 2, fixed or discretionary costs require a different method of control than do variable costs. They are controlled by conscious decisions on the part of managers. There is no automatic adjustment to changes in level of activity. However, this characteristic of fixed costs can be used to the firm's advantage. If an organization has an opportunity to bid on government contracts, incremental bidding could be very useful in maintaining the organization and contributing toward fixed expenses in bad times, particularly if the government business is separable from the firm's usual product markets. If government business is a permanent part of the firm's volume, then it may not be able to take advantage of this opportunity. However, because bids on one contract are not necessarily binding on another, the firm may be able to sell to the government in areas in which it has not sold before. Incremental pricing is extremely useful for contracts which are used as fill-ins for firms which do not do an extensive government business.

Market Segmentation and Incremental Pricing

When using incremental pricing, the firm should re-examine all markets. The firm's market within the United States should be segmented because particular territories may be more amenable to incremental pricing than others. There may be opportunities where incremental pricing will not spoil the market in the future. However, if the domestic market does not support the use of incremental pricing, the firm should not overlook the foreign market.

Even if the firm does not normally sell in the foreign market, in bad times it may be a lucrative market for use of incremental pricing. It will not necessarily mean the firm has to develop foreign expertise or hire foreign salesmen. Sales may be made through a broker or exporter. Although there are rules and agreements in international trade concerning product dumping (which is pricing below the domestic market for the purpose of dumping products in foreign markets) these may not be a barrier. The rules concerning dumping do not apply to all markets and are subject to interpretation. It is not difficult to estimate the risk of being accused of dumping and whether the threat is more imagined than real. The point, however, is that incrementalism can apply not only to products, but also to segmented markets by types of business and geography.

Eight Decision-Making Examples of Incremental Analysis Applications

Exhibit 12 is an example of the incremental analysis of a decision to replace a product with a new model of the same type. This analysis compares the current product's costs with the incremental sales and costs needed to introduce the new model. The development of the new model was approved because the incremental net income after taxes and the incremental discounted cash flow return from sales of the new model exceeded the targets required for projects of this type. This analysis, because of the return, also ranked high on the list of projects competing for funds. Both the marketing need for a new and better tool and the financial need for an adequate return on investment were met through this proposal. However, it was the analytical technique which emphasized the information needed for the decision!

Exhibit 13 is an analysis of the substitution of computer-prepared payroll summaries for manual summaries. These are examples of trading on internal fixed costs through the use of incremental costing to increase profits. The types of decisions to which incremental costing is applicable are too numerous to be listed in this chapter. However, some examples of the types of decisions for which incremental costing is useful are discussed in the next paragraphs. Should a manager be faced with any of these decisions, this list can be useful for identifying when to use incremental cost comparisons.

(1) *The hiring of additional salesmen.* This decision requires the measurement of the incremental costs of a salesman, such as his travel, salary, fringe benefits, plus any increase in administrative costs, and deducting the total from the income generated by the salesman's sales. From net sales generated by the salesman are deducted his incremental expenses including the variable costs of the products he will sell. If there is a contribution to fixed costs and profits and there are no other more acceptable alternatives, then the hiring of the salesmen is a good decision. Again, it must be emphasized that all risks must be evaluated; including the probability of not meeting the sales volume. There should be a range of alternatives with the choice made by a judgment of which of the alternatives is most likely to be achieved.

> An appliance producer computes incremental contribution for each salesman in each territory in the United States. This information is used for evaluating salesmen as well as determining pricing policy in his territory. As a result, a very effective sales force is maintained that must reach very high performance standards. Because of the performance of the sales force, this manufacturer has an extremely good reputation in its industry and continually takes share of market from its competitors.

(2) *New product introductions.* This is illustrated in Exhibit 12.

(3) *Product discontinuance.* The net sales of the product minus variable expenses is the method to use to determine whether the product should be discontinued and thus whether there is a contribution to fixed costs and profit. If there is no contribution, then the product should be discontinued. However, if the product is contributing to fixed costs and no other product will absorb that contribution, then discon-

tinuance is a poor decision. The period of measurement must be the future and not the past. The past can be used as a basis to predict the future; but, the analysis must be forward looking. If the product is not going to contribute to profits in the long run, then plans should be made for the introduction of another product to replace it or to phase it out as its contribution decreases.

> A clothing manufacturer dropped one particular model of a garment from his product line. The result was an increase in the cost of manufacturing the remaining models. Analysis indicated that the discontinued model was making a contribution to discretionary overhead and to profit after deducting the incremental costs of producing it. The overhead absorbed by this model had to be allocated to the remaining models after it was discontinued. Sales of the remaining models did not materially increase and this manufacturer was "worse off" after dropping that particular model. His overhead remained the same and his profit decreased!

(4) *Plant closings.* Often the decision to close manufacturing plants is based upon the total costs of operating the plant. If the plant can't be sold, however, and only the costs of maintaining it can be recovered by continuing operation, then the plant should remain in operation. If, however, the plant is not recovering the incremental costs of keeping it open, the plant should be closed.

> One company caught in a declining market had to choose between two plants. Production was sufficient to support only one plant. One plant was modern and new, the other older and fully depreciated. Analysis of the contribution above incremental costs indicated the new plant should be closed. The manufacturer closed that plant and survived the decline in his market! Sales slipped, but profits remained high!

(5) *Inventory reductions.* The incremental inventory carrying costs must be compared to the costs of replacing the inventory at some future date. The basic problem is to decide whether to repurchase the inventory or bear the costs of carrying it. In an analysis such as this, the cost of the current inventory is a sunk cost and not relevant.

> Leslie plastics discovered that it had a year's supply of a particular inventory. Analysis of carrying costs revealed

that the incremental costs of holding the inventory for a year less the proceeds from disposal exceeded the costs of replacing the inventory one year later. This was true despite the prediction of a slight price increase for that inventory item within the year. The analysis included insurance, interest, profit forgone because the money invested in inventory is not available for other uses, and variable warehousing costs. The original cost of the inventory was a sunk cost and therefore not applicable to this analysis.

(6) *The use of automation.* The incremental costs of automation should be related to the out-of-pocket costs of current operations, not the total costs! Only those costs which will actually be reduced or eliminated are considered savings. For example, the costs of the rental of the computer (if time based) are not relevant, nor are the savings in costs of supervision applicable unless supervisors are actually terminated.

A manufacturer who ignored these cost distinctions missed many opportunities to increase efficiency and increase cash flow. When deciding whether or not to automate clerical operations this manufacturer always includes an hourly cost for use of the central processing unit as part of the costs of automation even though the rental costs for this unit are fixed per month (time based). The result is cash outflow for the salaries of unneeded clerical employees and an under-utilized central processing unit.

(7) *Machine replacements.* In this case, the incremental savings from the acquisition of a new machine are compared to the incremental costs of purchasing, installing, and operating the new machine. As an example, the depreciation on the machine is only relevant to the evaluation to the extent it reduces taxes and thereby increases cash flow. In addition, the value of the increased production from the use of the new equipment, if any, is the incremental increase in cash flow.

An organization which continually updated its equipment through incremental cost and revenue analysis found itself with the most modern equipment in its industry. To take advantage of the high productivity of this equipment, this manufacturer lowered prices, took share of market from, and almost bankrupted, its competitors. Its strong market

> position led to an average annual profit growth rate of 15 percent.

(8) *Volume versus price tradeoffs.* Incrementalism is important when evaluating product price reductions. The incremental costs incurred initiating the reduction and the effect upon unit sales are keys to the evaluation of price reductions. The central question is whether a price reduction will generate enough additional volume to make a net contribution to profit and fixed costs. Again, this decision is dependent upon the incremental effect and not upon the application or allocation of fixed costs.

> One progressive firm developed a highly sophisticated computer model which analyzed changes in sales prices and quantities sold from these budgeted for each month and cumulative to date for the fiscal year. For each major product they could see the effects of a change in price upon quantity sold. From this analysis they were able to adjust prices and the manufacturing schedule as quickly as possible, to take advantage of incremental pricing. They "managed" their product mix to reach the largest profit possible under the circumstances.

Important Points to Remember About Incremental Costing

Incremental costing is an extremely useful tool for maximizing profits. It can: (a) contribute to survival of the firm in "bad times"; (b) increase profits through taking advantage of fixed costs; (c) increase productivity and efficiency; (d) contribute to maintenance of the human organization; (e) increase market share; and (f) increase a firm's knowledge about its cost structure and marketing environment.

The advantages of incrementalism become evident in the most important function of a business—to make a profit. The best test is to apply incremental costing to the business firm and reap the rewards of increased profits. At a minimum, incremental costing will help maintain profit margins, regardless of how bad the business environment is!

EXHIBIT 12

INCREMENTAL ANALYSIS
REPLACEMENT OF A PRODUCT
(000)

Description	Proposed Tool $	Proposed Tool %	Present Tool $	Present Tool %	Difference (Incremental Change) $	Difference (Incremental Change) %
Sales (3 Year Volume)	1,651	100.0	1,172	100.0	479	100.0
Estimated Manufacturing Costs (except for present Tool which is actual)	690	41.7	518	44.1	173	35.9
Projected Tool-Up Costs	36	2.1	—	—	36	7.5
Total Cost Of Sales	726	43.9	518	44.1	209	43.4
Gross Margin	925	56.0	654	55.9	270	56.6
Estimated Development Cost	17	.8	—	—	17	2.9
Variable General & Administrative Expenses	22	1.3	15	1.3	6	1.3
Estimated Contribution Margin (except for present Tool)	886	53.8	639	54.6	247	52.4
Discretionary General & Administrative Expenses	247	14.9	247	21.1	—	—
Income Before Taxes	639	38.9	392	33.5	247	52.4
Deduct Income Taxes	357	21.5	218	18.5	139	28.9
Net Income After Income Taxes	282	17.4	174	15.0	108	23.2
Discounted Cash Flow Return		+30.4		+33.2		+27.4

Note: The purpose of the analysis is to evaluate the introduction of a product redesign. The replacement product is evaluated on the basis of the effect of the changes it causes. There is an increase in sales volume as well as an increase in manufacturing costs. The replacement product will require an investment in tooling and development and an increase in Variable General and Administrative Expenses. However, the replacement product will increase net income after taxes by $108,000. The replacement product did not require any additional expenditures for fixed general and administrative costs. The analysis emphasizes what will change.

EXHIBIT 13

AUTOMATING THE GATHERING OF PAYROLL DATA (INCREMENTAL ANALYSIS)

(000)

Description	Amount	Cash Outflow	Cash Inflow	Net Cash Flow () Denotes Minus
Three Year Volume Savings				
Plant Payroll Clerks 2 per plant for 7 plants = 14 @ ($7,000 per year × 120% to include fringe benefits) $8,400 = × 3 years	$352,800		$352,800	$352,800
Reduction in Repairs to Plant Accounting Machines —average of 5 repairs per year at $100 per repair × 3 years	$ 1,500		$ 1,500	$ 1,500
Reduction in Accounting Machines in Plants 14 × $6,000 = $84,000 × 3 years	$252,000	No effect—this is a sunk cost		
Reduction in square feet of Plant devoted to office space, 1,400 square feet @ $20 per square feet × 3 years	$ 84,000	No effect upon the analysis—this is a sunk cost		
Costs				
Expenses incurred to develop the computer program to process piece work tickets. One time purchase.	$ 20,000	$ 20,000		($20,000)
Data Conversion—Costs of purchasing outside service for converting data to machine readable form. $1,000 per week for 52 weeks $52,000 × 3 years	$156,000	$156,000		($156,000)
Forms, paper & data processing cards $3,000 per year × 3 years	$ 1,560	Not used in the analysis because this cost could be incurred regardless of the change in the system.		
Net change in cash flow		$185,000	$354,300	+$169,300

This analysis is illustrative of the use of incremental costs for the purpose of making decisions. This example was taken from an analysis used by a firm with a complicated piece-work payroll. Through substituting the use of the computer, a fixed and sunk cost, for that of labor (payroll clerks), this company increased its cash flow and thus its profits. This analysis emphasizes only those costs affected by the decision; i.e., those that will change. The decision was to use the computer and take advantage of the savings!

Chapter 6

Cost Reduction Reporting

Key to a Successful Cost Reduction Program

Cost reduction programs are often thought of as being initiated when economic conditions are unfavorable or used to reduce costs when sales decrease. However, a successful cost reduction program is continuous. It is as important in good as in bad times. The program is not used to reduce costs to coincide with shrinking sales, but involves decreasing costs to increase profit and capture share of market. Its continuous use makes the program more acceptable to employees than a sudden crash effort in response to an adverse economy. Also, the continuous record of each group's performance is available for evaluation. This record is useful for setting future cost reduction objectives and for measuring contribution to the firm's profits.

Businesses tend to be lax during economic booms, but continuing cost reduction programs are a vital necessity to the economic health of the firm! Remember! Every dollar saved through cost reduction is a dollar of profit!

> One extremely profitable organization has a continuous and well organized cost reduction program. It is strongly adhered to and supported by top management in good times as well as bad. This manufacturer is known for its history of growth in earnings. Its cost reduction effort is an important contributor to that record. Approximately 20 percent of its before-tax profit is a result of the cost reduction program.

Six Clear-cut Benefits of Cost Reduction Reporting

1. Cost reduction reporting supports the need for adjustments to meet goals not on target.
2. It keeps management informed of progress against objectives.
3. Each manager knows his contribution and that of his employees to the success or failure of the cost reduction program.
4. It arouses the interest of managers and employees.
5. All employees will be aware of the accomplishments and the benefits of a cost reduction program.
6. Continuous reporting emphasizes goals which are being exceeded and points out those that are not being met.

Objective Setting to Insure Success

One prime ingredient of a cost reduction program is objective setting. How the objectives are set will determine the emphasis the program receives from the organization's employees.

The first step for determining the detail cost reduction objectives is to set the overall organizational goal. A logical approach is to estimate the total of all wage increases to be granted in the coming fiscal year. This estimate becomes one cost to be offset through the cost reduction program.

In addition, all expected materials price increases must be forecast as part of the cost reduction goal. Usually the labor cost increases can be estimated by the financial department with some input from the industrial relations department and historical information. The estimated material cost increases must come from the purchasing department and be coordinated with the production schedule. Additionally, all anticipated increases in the cost of fringe benefits are included in the goal. The total of the increases in these three costs equals the overall cost reduction objective. This is a tentative objective for the firm, keeping in mind, however, that it will not be final until it is thoroughly reviewed.

Nerak Corporation traditionally sets its cost reduction objective as the recovery of all estimated inflationary in-

> creases in costs in the next fiscal year. This broad objective is then further defined into specific projects; through these projects the firm usually reaches its goal. The cost reduction program contributes over one million dollars annually to profits before taxes.

The Importance of Communication

It should be understood that while setting the cost reduction objectives, the necessary contacts within and communication of the goals throughout the organization must be used to reinforce the awareness of the value of the cost reduction program. Employees can easily be taught to identify cost reduction projects. Two-way communication can result in the acceptance of cost reduction as a way of life and an everyday event. One method of communication is to relate the cost reduction program to the need to be competitive and the effect of taking share of market upon job security. It can also be related to the use of the savings from the program, for example, for wage increases for contributing employees.

> To encourage participation, a contractor has a policy of rewarding participating employees and their managers by sharing the savings from the cost reduction program with them. The employees share is usually a percent of the savings for a particular period of time, the percentage and time period being agreed upon by the company and the employee. The result has been well compensated employees and a cost savings of over 10 million in the last 5 years.

Who Should Participate in the Determination of the Cost Reduction Objectives

Without the full support of the very top managers of the organization, cost reduction will fail. These top managers must support and take the leadership in keeping cost reduction programs viable. In addition to supporting the program themselves, they must convince the managers of the organization subdivisions of the value and the need for the program. It is not sufficient to order subdivision managers to support the program; they must be convinced. The success of the program depends upon the identification of projects by which cost reduction objectives can be met and this process is highly dependent upon the contribution of managers throughout the organization.

> The cost reduction process each fiscal year in one large supplier of machinery begins with a meeting of the president of the company and each division head and his subdivision managers. At this meeting the president openly discusses the purpose of the cost reduction program and what the overall plan is. After this meeting and other meetings throughout the organization the top management of the company, i.e., the division vice-presidents and the president get together to discuss and summarize the results. Usually, there are more cost reduction projects identified than there are resources to complete them. Middle managers compete to be the largest contributor to the cost reduction program.

The Process of Determining Cost Reduction Objectives

After meeting with various groups throughout the organization, the chief executive officer, all the vice-presidents and the chief financial officer meet to set the tentative objective for the whole organization. This may be an absolute number or a range. Generally, it will be based upon the labor, material and fringe benefit increases which are to be offset through the cost reduction program. At this meeting the objective is viewed as a tentative goal. It must be remembered that the execution of the program is dependent upon the identification of specific detailed projects. At this point in the development of the program these projects are unknown.

This meeting could be called a strategy meeting, in which the contemplated cost increases are related to the pricing strategy needed to support the specific marketing objectives. This is discussed in detail for specific markets and products. The ability of the organization to meet its profit objectives is examined. If the cost reduction program is not sufficient to meet these profit objectives, alternatives, such as modification of the program or re-evaluation of the marketing goals, are considered.

> The desire not to increase product prices motivates a very profitable company to follow this procedure each year for determining its cost reduction objectives. Each year it more than offsets its cost increases and takes share of market. Without the cost reduction program, this company estimates its net income after taxes would be reduced at least 25 percent and it could not have achieved the 10 percent annual growth in profits that it has had for the past 12 years.

The Influence of Competition

The strategies of competitors are an important input to the cost reduction program. If competitors are expected to increase prices, the firm's cost reduction plan will be affected. Cost reduction goals may exclude some inflationary cost increases if these can be recovered through price increases. On the other hand, if the strategy is to take a larger share of market, cost reductions must be planned to recover more than inflationary costs. An estimate of what competitor's reactions will be is an important part of the plan!

The Dissemination of the Objectives

After a strategy meeting with the president, the head of each division, such as the Vice-President for Personnel, Vice-President for Manufacturing, and the Vice-President for Engineering hold similar meetings with their key managers and employees. The purpose is to review the organizations overall cost reduction objective. The vice-president discusses with his people that portion of the objective to be assumed by his division. Again, this is an assumption of a portion of the overall company objective by a single division. It is a working objective, but not yet the cost reduction program for that division.

The managers and key people of each division will identify projects and areas where savings can be made. From the identification of these projects the division heads and their key people will compute a cost reduction goal for the division. The results of this computation are compared to the objectives adopted on a tentative basis. If there is agreement between the two objectives, the division program is set. If not, the division must choose one of the objectives. If it is decided to adopt the original objective chosen by the firm's top managers, then a division plan for accomplishing that objective is developed and disseminated. If not, the plan chosen must be discussed throughout the division and the head of the division must inform top management of the need to modify the division objective.

After the division meeting between the heads of finance, manufacturing, engineering, etc., and their managers, each plant, product, and staff manager meets with his key people. The purpose is to review the portion of the overall objective which each can accept. In this meeting, the division and subdivision objectives will be distributed among the various plants and staff departments. The distribution is based upon judgment as to what cost reductions each area can achieve. Then, each plant and staff manager is asked to identfy specific cost reduction projects with which to accomplish the goal assigned.

Before the meeting adjourns, a date is set for presentation and review of the detail projects. When the meeting reconvenes, the specific projects are identified and their total is compared to the cost reduction objective for that subdivision. If the specific project totals equal or exceed the overall objective then the tentative objective is accepted as the subdivision goal. If the specific reductions identified are less than the portion of the goal assigned to that subdivision, the projects which have been selected and identified are reviewed again. If it is decided that the subdivision cannot meet the tentative objective assigned, this decision is communicated to the top managers and the cost reduction objective is reduced to conform with that identified through specific projects.

If the project totals identified exceed the tentative objective, the objective is accepted and the possible excess is reported to the firm's top managers. They may wish to revise the objectives or keep these projects "in the bank" for future use.

A successful management team may, as in at least one case, use two sets of objectives for cost reduction. One is a minimum goal to accomplish the organizations committed profit objective. The other is the optimum which they hope to achieve, but to which too much uncertainty attaches to be adapted as a firm commitment. If the optimum goal were used when planning, the probability of accomplishing the profit target would be reduced and thereby management's credibility. By using the most achievable amount, the company's profit plan is highly reliable!

Assignment of the Responsibility for Meeting the Cost Reduction Objectives

When discussing the assignment of responsibility it is assumed that specific cost reduction projects have been identified by each division and subdivision of the firm and a total organization cost reduction objective has been agreed upon. This will result in some divisions and subdivisions having a smaller objective than was originally sought and others will have a larger objective. But nonetheless, an objective for each part and for the total organization has been agreed upon. The next step is to assign each project to an individual. This begins with the assignment of a group of projects to a manager such as that illustrated in Exhibit 14. Each project is identified with the manager's name at the level where the authority and resources exist for completing the project. In other words, the assignment must consider the manager's ability and authority to accomplish the objective. If he doesn't have the authority or the resources, he cannot be assigned that project.

Reporting on the Cost Reduction

In addition, the assignment carries a responsibility for periodic reporting such as the accounting department report illustrated in Exhibit 15. The manager is responsible not only for accomplishing the objective but also for periodic reporting on the progress towards the objective. However, the manager must have the support and assistance of the financial department for reporting, if needed. Usually reporting involves a detailed project report to the financial department for summarization and inclusion in the total company report. Additionally, the manager must review his report, in detail and in person, with his supervisor. Although finance issues a monthly report, it is not necessary that the manager meet monthly with his supervisor. He is not necessarily committed to a review of his progress each month with the next level of management. They may choose to review the cost reduction report every second month, every third month, or on some other basis such as weekly. Whatever the manager's reporting responsibilities to the financial department, the arrangement with his supervisor is adjusted to their schedules and interests.

> One manufacturer issues monthly reports such as are illustrated in Exhibits #14, #15, #16, and #17, on all cost reduction programs. A report is prepared for each division of the company and a summary for the total organization. Each division report is reviewed by top management with the financial department, with division management and then with division employees. At any time, the top manager or the president of the company may discuss the progress or lack of it with groups of employees on a random basis. Because of the participation of the president, employees recognize the importance of the program and monitor their performance. The success of this program, with its contribution of millions of dollars in cost savings, is one of the reasons this company is listed in the top one-third of Fortune's Top 500 companies in profitability!

The Financial Department's Role as a Reporter

The financial department is responsible for issuing a cost reduction report to all levels of management on a basis consistent with the financial closing schedule. Exhibits 14, 15, 16 and 17 are examples of a typical cost reduction report. This is a monthly report which summarizes the results for the reporting month and for the fiscal year to date. In the report, the actual results are compared to the appropriate cost reduction plan on a basis which is consistent with the reporting sequence, i.e., month and year to date. Also, the results expected for the remainder of the budget year are reprojected for consistency with actuals to date and changes expected in the near future. However, the financial department cannot report without the cooperation of line management. With the help of line managers, a projection of what is to be expected for the remainder of the fiscal year, compared to the original objectives, can be prepared. The report must be summarized by division and company totals. Additionally, the report includes detailed schedules summarizing the actual costs for each project by subdivision, compared to the savings objective.

To illustrate the effect of the progress of the cost reduction program to date, the financial department prepared pro forma statements which reflect the financial condition at the end of the fiscal year. These statements emphasize the financial condition the organization will be in if it continues on its present course.

The detailed reporting provides a document which managers at all organization levels can use to assess their progress toward their goals. Generally, managers react by following up on projects which are falling behind, revising objectives, or substituting new projects with which to meet established goals. Any changes will be thoroughly discussed throughout the management hierarchy and new courses of action approved. When this process has been completed for the first month it will continue for the rest of the fiscal year with changing, reviewing, and resetting until the year is ended.

> One major supplier of equipment makes a detailed monthly report for each month of the fiscal year for each cost reduction project. The report is further summarized by subdivision, division and a total for the organization. The monthly review of this report is conducted by the chief financial officer at a meeting of the top management committee which is responsible for the day-to-day operation of the business. The effect of this meeting is top management involvement in the cost reduction program and an immediate adjustment by the organization to variations from plan. This company usually exceeds its objective and adds at least 10 percent to its bottom line each year through cost reductions!

Cost Reduction Reporting Should be Integrated with Audits of Financial Analysis and Break-Even Reporting

Cost reduction reporting should be integrated with auditing of financial analyses. The integration is necessary to verify that cost reductions associated with financial analyses are captured in the cost reduction report. The benefits identified in financial analyses should be included in the cost reduction program. In addition, the integration of these reports can have converse results. The cost reduction report may be proof of the success of a cost reduction included in a financial analysis. Some examples of the need for integration are the analysis of the substitution of one product for another and frozen standard reporting. The financial analysis of product substitution indicates the success or failure of the project; however, a copy of the financial analysis should be compared to the cost reduction report. Cost reductions were probably included in the calculation of savings from product redesign and should be included in the report. On the other hand, a financial analysis which included installation of a new system with reductions in the cost of personnel, material, and communications, would include in the proposal and the audit of the proposal, information useful for cost reduction reporting. The savings from the implementation of the new system should be included in the cost reduction report for the year in which the savings occurred.

Frozen standard reporting can also be integrated with cost reduction reporting. This integration is recommended for at least two reasons. One, to trace product cost reductions to verify that the cost reductions did result in a change in the standards. And two, to verify that decreases in the standards caused by cost reductions were included in the cost reduction report. If, for example, a savings was proposed that reduced manufacturing and warranty costs by reducing the number of parts in a tool, the cost reduction report should be used to trace the change through the standard cost report. The comparisons included in the frozen standard cost report would prove whether or not the cost reduction had indeed been accomplished. On the other hand, a change indicated on the frozen standard report should be traced to the cost reduction report to verify that the change was reported and included as a benefit in the cost reduction program.

For a variety of reasons it is necessary that cost reduction reporting be integrated with break-even reporting. For one, it is important that management know if cost reductions have affected fixed costs possibly lowering the break-even point. If this has resulted from certain cost reductions, management may want to take advantage of the lowered break-even point and make a downward adjustment in prices. Managers should know if they have more leeway from a change in costs to respond to adverse economic conditions or to accomplish other strategies. In addition, cost reduction projects which lower the break-even point should be given a relatively high priority and followed more closely. By identifying these projects in the cost reduction report, management can follow them more closely and use the cost reduction as additional input for revising the break-even point.

Exhibits

To illustrate the type of information needed for effective cost reduction reporting, the exhibits include examples of cost reduction reports for a manufacturing, engineering, energy and power, and accounting department as well as a consolidated report. Exhibit 14 is an example of a manufacturing department cost reduction report. It includes a number of different projects and a variety of methods for computing savings. This report is prepared monthly and is cumulative for the fiscal year with the objectives summarized similarly. The report includes the name of the manager responsible for each project and a definitive project description. Also included are the details of how the cost savings are computed.

An engineering department cost reduction report is illustrated in Exhibit 15. The report includes the redesign of some products, internal system redesigns, and other changes which should result in savings. This report is summarized by both results and objectives for the month and fiscal year. Note that the estimated life of the project is included in the description of the savings computation. This estimate supports the company's budgeting and planning process by providing estimates of future savings.

Exhibit 16 illustrates a cost reduction report for an accounting department. This is an example of the use of cost reduction reporting in a staff environment. This report is also summarized by month and fiscal year for the actual results, and the objectives.

Exhibit 17 is a cost reduction report for an energy and power department. With the rapid increases in energy costs, the survival of the firm depends on the least cost operation of this department. This report is summarized similarly to Exhibits 14, 15 and 16.

Exhibit 18 is an example of a cost reduction report for a transportation department. This report includes the goals and actual results for both the month and the fiscal year.

An example of a consolidated cost reduction report for the whole organization is included in Exhibit 19. This report is a summary of the reports for the various divisions and departments of the company. The actual results and objectives for the whole company are summarized by month and fiscal year.

EXHIBIT 14

MANUFACTURING COST REDUCTION REPORT FOR THE MONTH OF MARCH 19XX (Based upon Cash Savings)

( ) Indicates unfavorable variation from objective

Project Number	Description	Project start date / Project Manager	Method of Computing Savings	March actual savings	Month obj.	Month var.	FY to date actual	FY to date obj.	FY to date var.
XX-10	Replace machine X with machine Y at plant 3 section 12. (Note: In this case the parts flow through station 12 evenly throughout the year. This will not always be the case & savings must be computed accordingly.)	Feb. 15, 19XX William Johnson	Reduction in production costs per unit multiplied by number of units produced. This change is expected to have a 5-year life. Because of the use of accelerated depreciation, the savings per unit are greater in the early years. Total estimated savings *$100,000.*	2500	2500	—	3800	3800	—
XX-11	Install a Data Processing System to reduce investment in raw material and work in process inventories.	Feb. 1, 19XX Fred Fisher	Compute the difference between the inventories before and after the installation of the new system. To compute this difference any inventory increase caused by increased volume must be accounted for. The net dollar reduction in inventories is multiplied by the percent savings in working capital, insurance, warehousing, and handling. From this the incremental costs of design, installation, and operation of the new system must be deducted to arrive at net savings. Because the costs of designing and installing the new system occur early in the project, the savings are less in the early years. This change is expected to have a 5-year life. Total savings are estimated at *$250,000.*	2000	3000	(1000)	3000	5000	(2000)

EXHIBIT 14 (Continued)

MANUFACTURING COST REDUCTION REPORT

( ) Indicates unfavorable variation from objective

Project Number	Description	Project start date / Project Manager	Method of Computing Savings	March actual savings	Month obj.	Month var.	FY to date actual	FY to date obj.	FY to date var.
XX-12	Replace present gears with powdered metal gears for products G and H.	Jan. 1, 19XX / Leroy Long	Subtract the cost of the current machined gears from the estimated cost of the powdered metal gears and multiply the estimated savings per gear by the quantities of products G and H scheduled for manufacture. This change is expected to have a 3-year life. Total estimated savings are *$600,000.*	20,000	16,500	3500	60,000	49,500	10,500
XX-13	Revise the sequence of the assembly of subassembly NP, which reduces the labor content of each subassembly.	April 1, 19XX / Milton Kilroy	Multiply the net reduction in direct labor fractional hours for each NP assembly by the projected direct labor rate for the assembly department. Multiply this result by the number of NP assemblies expected to be manufactured. This change is expected to have a two-year life. Total savings are estimated at *$400,000.*	—	—	—	—	—	—
		Totals	$1,350,000	$24,500	$22,000	$2,500	$66,800	$85,800	$8,500

EXHIBIT 15

DEVELOPMENT ENGINEERING COST REDUCTION REPORT FOR THE MONTH OF MARCH 19XX (Based upon Cash Savings)

( ) Indicates unfavorable variation from objective

Project Number	Description	Project start date / Project Manager	Method of Computing Savings	March actual savings	Month obj.	Month var.	FY to date actual	FY to date obj.	FY to date var.
XX-23	Redesign Product M to reduce the number of parts from 22 to 15.	January 1, 19XX Charles Blair	Savings are computed by deducting the cost of the seven parts eliminated from the cost of product M and comparing the costs of manufacturing the scheduled quantities of product M before the elimination of the parts with the cost after. This redesign is expected to have a life of 3 years. The total estimated savings is *$300,000.*	7000	8300	(1300)	26,000	24,900	1100
XX-24	Substitute computer and plotter for design labor to go from model to templates and finished drawings.	January 1, 19XX Tom Jeffers	Compute the number of design laborers to be terminated because of the purchase and installation of the new equipment. The savings will be less at first because of the need to invest in equipment and the learning time required to use the equipment effectively. This change is expected to have a life of 5 years. The total estimated savings is *$500,000*	—	—	—	(20,000)	(20,000)	—
XX-25	Test product life on a computer and eleminate the need for two test employees, their overtime, and fringe benefits.	March 1, 19XX Bill Stitely	Compute the yearly wages, average overtime and the fringe benefits saved by eliminating the two test positions. The cost of programming the test must be deducted from these savings. The computer is already "in house" and has excess capacity.						

EXHIBIT 15 (Continued)

DEVELOPMENT ENGINEERING COST REDUCTION REPORT

Project Number	Description	Project Manager / Project start date	Method of Computing Savings	March actual savings	Month obj.	Month var.	FY to date actual	FY to date obj.	FY to date var.
XX-25	(Continued)		This procedure is expected to last two years. The total estimated savings is *$25,000.*	1,000	1,000	—	1,000	1,000	—
XX-26	Replace drawing file of parts by numbers with file based upon configuration.	February 1, 19XX Roland Bavis	This change is estimated to speed up the period of parts redesign and thereby allow design changes to reach the market faster. It is estimated that redesigns will reach the market six months earlier. 75% of redesigns are for cost savings or new products rather than customers convenience. The life of this project is the maximum permitted, 5 years. The total estimated savings is *$165,000.*	2,000	3,000	(1,000)	5,000	6,000	(1,000)
			Totals $990,000	$10,000	$12,300	(2,300)	$12,000	$11,900	$100

EXHIBIT 16

ACCOUNTING DEPARTMENT COST REDUCTION REPORT FOR THE MONTH OF MARCH 19XX (Based upon Cash Savings)

( ) Indicates unfavorable variation from objective

Project Number	Description	Project start date / Project Manager	Method of Computing Savings	March actual savings	Month obj.	Month var.	FY to date actual	FY to date obj.	FY to date var.
XX-31	The automation of the cost accounting system for WW plant. The gathering of data and cost reporting is currently manual. (Note: The savings do not flow evenly because of the design and programming costs in the first year.)	January 1, 19XX Aldos Leidig	The costs of designing, programming, and storing the automated system on a time-share computer plus the costs of renting and running time on a time-share terminal were deducted from the savings caused by the elimination of two clerks salaries and fringe benefits. Estimated life of the project is three years. The total estimated savings are *$26,000.*	600	500	100	1,600	1,500	100
XX-32	Replacement of the present copying machine with a machine which offers the same features at less base rental and cost per copy.	January 1, 19XX Gilbert Higgins	Multiply the savings in rental per month and the savings per copy times the number of months of the project life and the number of copies expected to be run. (There is no difference in the paper or other supply costs between the two copiers.) The projects estimated useful life is 5 years. Total estimated savings is *$50,000.*	700	840	(140)	2,600	2,520	80
XX-33	Automate the payment of vendors invoices through the purchase of an accounts payable system.	February 1, 19XX Earl Brown	The savings in salary and fringe benefits are adjusted for the costs of the system plus any incremental costs of running the payables. These costs include any programming modifications but not equipment costs. The useful life of the project is estimated at 5 years. The total estimated savings are *$60,000.*	1,000	1,000	—	2,000	2,000	—

EXHIBIT 16 (Continued)

ACCOUNTING DEPARTMENT COST REDUCTION REPORT

Project Number	Description	Project Manager / Project start date	Method of Computing Savings	March actual savings	Month obj.	Month var.	FY to date actual	FY to date obj.	FY to date var.
XX-34	The reorganization of the credit department to add one credit analyst and increase the receivables turn by 5.	March 1, 19XX Gilbert Hibberd	Deduct the salary and fringe benefit cost of one analyst from the estimated increase in return on capital caused by the increase in turn of the accounts receivable. This project has an estimated life of 5 years. The total estimated savings are *$225,000.*	4,000	3,600	400	4,000	3,600	400
			Totals $361,000	$6,300	$5,940	$360	$10,200	$9,620	$580

EXHIBIT 17

ENERGY AND POWER DEPARTMENT COST REDUCTION REPORT FOR THE MONTH OF MARCH 19XX (Based upon Cash Savings)

( ) Indicates unfavorable variation from objective

Project Number	Description	Project Manager / Project start date	Method of Computing Savings	March actual savings	Month obj.	Month var.	FY to date actual	FY to date obj.	FY to date var.
XX-41	Computerize switching of all electrical equipment	February 1, 19XX Joseph Weaver	Savings are computed by comparing the electric utility invoices for usage before and after the installation of the computers. The usage savings multiplied by the standard rate equals the total savings. This change is expected to have a life of 3 years. The total savings is estimated at *$1,500,000.*	$10,000	$15,000	($5,000)	$20,000	$20,000	—
XX-42	Re-insulating outside walls sealing 50% of windows in all factories.	March 1, 19XX Bob Jaffin	The flow metering of the usage of steam before and after the change is the basis for computing the quantity saved. This quantity will be multiplied by a standard rate to calculate the savings. This project has a life of 3 years. The total estimated savings are *$500,000.*	$ 2,000	$ 1,000	$1,000	$ 2,000	$ 1,000	$1,000
XX-43	Resealing all doors, except two at each facility, for emergency use only.	March 1, 19XX Charles Powers	Draft readings will be taken at each door before and after it is sealed. From these readings the heat or air conditioning savings will be computed. This project has a life of 3 years. The total estimated savings are *$250,000.*	—	$ 3,000	($3,000)	—	$ 3,000	($3,000)
			Totals $2,250,000	$12,000	$19,000	($7,000)	$22,000	$24,000	($2,000)

EXHIBIT 18

TRANSPORTATION DEPARTMENT COST REDUCTION REPORT
FOR THE MONTH OF MARCH 19XX
(Based upon Cash Savings)

( ) Indicates unfavorable variation from objective

Project Number	Description	Project Manager / Project start date	Method of Computing Savings	March actual savings	Month obj.	Month var.	FY to date actual	FY to date obj.	FY to date var.
XX-51	Switching from rail to truck for transporting livestock.	January 1, 19XX Bill Daby	Savings are computed by comparing the difference in livestock lost in transit less the increase in transportation cost. This change is expected to have a life of 5 years. The total savings is estimated at *$300,000.*	$ 5,000	$ 5,000	—	$16,000	$15,000	$1,000
XX-52	Re-structuring route to eliminate two drivers.	January 1, 19XX John Hill	Savings are computed by adding the savings in salary plus savings in fringe benefit costs. This change is expected to have a life of 3 years. The total savings is estimated at *$150,000.*	$ 6,000	$ 5,000	$1,000	$16,000	$14,000	$2,000
			Totals $450,000	$11,000	$10,000	$1,000	$32,000	$29,000	$3,000

EXHIBIT 19

FOR THE MONTH OF MARCH 19XX
(Based upon Cash Savings)

( ) Indicates unfavorable variation from objective

Project Number	Description	Project Manager / Project start date	Method of Computing Savings	March actual savings	Month obj.	Month var.	FY to date actual	FY to date obj.	FY to date var.
Various	Manufacturing Department Cost Reduction Report	Various	See detailed report attached. $1,350,000	$24,500	$22,000	$2,500	$ 66,800	$ 58,300	$ 8,500
Various	Development Engineering Cost Reduction Report	Various	See detailed report attached. $990,000	10,000	12,000	(2,300)	12,000	11,900	100
Various	Accounting Department Cost Reduction Report	Various	See detailed report attached. $361,000	6,300	5,940	360	10,200	9,620	580
Various	Energy and Power Department Cost Reduction Report	Various	See detailed report attached. $2,250,000	12,000	19,000	(7,000)	22,000	24,000	(2,000)
Various	Transportation Department Cost Reduction Report	Various	See detailed report attached. $450,000	11,000	10,000	1,000	32,000	29,000	3,000
			Report Totals $5,401,000	$63,800	$69,240	$5,440	$143,000	$132,820	$10,180

Chapter 7

Controlling the Cost of Support Departments, Such as Data Processing and Maintenance, Through Zero Based Budgeting

The Advantage of Zero Based Budgeting of Data Processing

As the importance of data processing increases and as it uses more of an organization's resources, it is necessary to assure the firm's managers of an adequate return on this investment. Investments in data processing are extremely costly—central processing units can cost up to five hundred thousand dollars each for a medium-sized application and hardware and software support require an additional investment of the firm's resources.

Zero based budgeting is an efficient and useful method for controlling data processing costs and an effective tool for guaranteeing that data processing will contribute to profitability and justify the large investment required. The use of zero based budgeting reduces waste and causes a larger return than is usual from the investment in data processing because data processing must be efficient to succeed.

A Major Advantage of Zero Based Budgeting Is It Discourages Empire Building

Because most line managers are not intimately familiar with the language and method of operations, the data processing organization is not closely supervised. In addition, the uniqueness of its methods, the "buzz" words and use of unfamiliar equipment tend to encourage the building of an almost autonomous empire. The empire is not only built upon more programmers and systems analysts, usually with fewer programs written and systems implemented, but also with more and larger equipment without a detailed justification for the expense.

Zero based budgeting prevents wasting this valuable resource because those parts of the firm with the largest potential return from using data processing will be the first to get data processing services. The "ivory tower" mentality of data processing is eliminated and data processing is forced to adopt a user-oriented approach to problems. Data processing is forced to convince users of the advantages of its services over manual or other methods.

Additionally, the potential user must justify the purchase of data processing services. When the user wishes to take advantage of these services, he must estimate the financial and other effects upon his organization. If the estimated results are not satisfactory, then the user chooses another alternative. However, there must be follow-up to check the actual results achieved. If anticipated savings were not realized, the causes should be investigated and understood. The firm's objectives are to take advantage of all possible savings.

Zero based budgeting requires continual and intensive interaction between users and data processing. This promotes cooperation and an understanding within the whole firm of the purpose, function, and use of data processing. It also forces data processing to integrate its objectives with those of the whole firm.

> One multi-product firm zero-base-budgets its central data processing group which provides services for most of its operating divisions and plants. The data processing cost system is computerized and is the source of actual charges to users as well as the origin of estimates used for bidding on projects. Zero based budgeting has successfully elimi-

nated duplication of effort and the waste of data processing services throughout the firm. Within one operating division of the firm, zero based budgeting saved approximately $175,000 of cash flow per year.

How to Zero-Base-Budget Data Processing Effectively

The first step needed to zero-base-budget the data processing division is to prepare an organization chart of all the sections and operations within data processing. This chart must include all of data processing and must group functions within data processing which relate to one another. This is the basis for cost control. The costs for each section of data processing to be accumulated include employees' salaries, fringe benefits, supervision, physical facilities and equipment, and various supplies and expenses. The following groups are usually found within a typical data processing operation:

1. *Computer Operations* — which consist of computer operators, the central processing unit and related equipment used for output from the computer.
2. *New Systems Programming* — this involves programmers who program new systems.
3. *The Systems Analyst Section* — included here are the costs of those employees who create the flow chart systems, rather than those who translate them into machine language.
4. *Operational Programming* — which includes the cost of programmers who support the computer operations. The nature of the costs included in this section must be strictly limited to those who modify project programs or edit control programs for the specific purpose of making the most efficient use of the central processing unit and other peripheral equipment. It does not include maintenance programming.
5. *Maintenance Programmers* — these are programmers who update existing system programs, which must be modified because of changes in operations. Mainte-

nance programmers are differentiated from new systems programmers who program only new systems which are developed from changes in data processing technology as it matures and changes in the firm's operating methods.

6. Many data processing installations have a *planning and equipment evaluation section.* The function of this group is to plan for the future needs and applications of data processing. In addition, this group evaluates the need for modification and substitution of equipment as data processing applications change.
7. Almost all data processing organizations have a *data conversion section.* Included in this section are key punch machine operators, key-to-disc operators, supervisors, key punch machines, and key-to-disc equipment.
8. The general management of data processing includes the *top managers of the data processing organization* and their staffs. It includes the division manager of data processing, his clerical support and any staff assistants that he might have.

One NYSE manufacturer has organized his data processing group in this fashion to focus the attention of his data processors on objectives. They must seek and satisfy users. In one application involving a minimum use of their resources, they saved the company in excess of $60,000 in cash over a period of two years. Without zero based budgeting, this job probably would have been deemed too small to bother with.

Cost Center Identification Is Necessary for Zero Based Budgeting

After each group within data processing has been defined and identified on the organization chart, the financial division must assign a cost center number to each section for cost collection and identification purposes. The cost center number includes one digit which identifies data processing and a series of subset numbers applicable to each section of data processing as outlined on the organization chart. The cost center is the tool by which costs are accumulated for each group within data processing and it is used for allocating the accumulated costs either to other data processing groups or to other departments using data processing services.

The cost center account numbers are assigned to facilitate grouping for further processing. A most useful and convenient classification system is to group the cost centers by type of costs, i.e., direct and indirect. The cost centers in which direct charges are accumulated are allocated differently from indirect cost centers. The costs accumulated in direct cost centers are transferred to user departments as direct charges for services performed.

Allocation of Direct Costs

The costs accumulated in direct cost centers are allocated to users based upon direct contact with their data requirements, such as costs for programs processed on the computer equipment are allocated by hours of computer running time. The salaries and fringe benefits of new systems programmers are direct costs of new systems and are allocated to new systems based upon the programming hours used. The costs of systems analysts are allocated to existing systems and new systems by the number of analyst hours used on each. The direct costs of maintenance programmers are allocated to each program revised, on the basis of programming hours consumed by the revision.

The direct costs, i.e., salaries and fringe benefits of key punch and key-to-disc operators are identified with each batch or group of input which is processed for each system or job. In addition, the depreciation or lease costs of the conversion equipment are identified with the machine hours required for each job as part of that job's direct costs. The lease costs or depreciation charges for the central processing unit and its peripheral equipment are also direct charges to users. These costs are allocated by the central processing unit hours required to process each job.

Each job processed by data processing must be assigned a job, identification, or project number. This number is used to collect and transfer the direct costs of each data processing section to users as the user's project is processed by that section of data processing. Each project number identifies the nature of the job and the user to be charged for the processing costs.

Indirect Costs in Direct Cost Centers

Indirect cost accumulation accounts are established to accumulate the salaries and fringe benefits of section managers and supervisors, salaries and fringe benefits of clerical support in each section, and supplies, rent and utilities applicable to each section of data processing. These indirect costs are allocated to projects as a percentage of the direct charges to each project processed in that section. Therefore, each project which is processed through a direct cost center will be allocated a portion of the center's overhead or indirect costs.

Indirect Cost Centers

In addition to the indirect costs in direct cost centers, there are cost centers that cannot be identified to projects and, therefore, must be totally allocated as indirect costs to users. Operational programming is one cost center that cannot be identified with projects. The best allocation procedure is to charge these costs to users as a percentage of the direct labor dollars of computer operators transferred to each project.

The planning and equipment evaluation section is also an indirect cost center. The costs incurred for operating this center are transferred to the other direct data processing cost centers based upon the total costs incurred in the direct centers. These costs become a part of the direct cost center's indirect costs and are allocated to projects as a percentage of labor dollars.

Another indirect cost center is the cost center used for the collection of the general management costs of data processing. The costs accumulated in this center are transferred to all other data processing cost centers, including indirect cost centers, based upon the total cost incurred in each center. These costs are then reallocated to other direct and indirect cost centers, projects, and thus to users.

Cost centers are a convenient way of accumulating the actual costs incurred by data processing for allocation. However, there are a number of methods for charging users. One method is to transfer costs to the users' projects based upon a budgeted rate multiplied by the actual hours required each month by each project. But, if this method is used, the rates must be adjusted to actual at least at the end of each quarter or year.

Many companies use this method because the actual costs for data processing are not known each month until after the closing of the financial records. An alternative is to close the data processing records ahead of the rest of the organization and thereby adjust the rates to actual each month. By closing the data processing records early, users are charged for services at the actual hours used multiplied by the actual labor, expense and overhead rates. There is no need for an adjustment in rates later in the year.

The use of cost centers is important not only as a tool for allocating charges to users, but to establish an historical base from which future budgets for data processing are prepared. Also, the historical information is needed as a source for preparing cost estimates for each project undertaken or bid upon. These control or cost center numbers are also a vehicle by which the data processing cost system can be mechanized and processed on the computer.

> A food processor organized its central data processing services by this method and replaced the divisional data processing organization with services from the central unit. The central cost system is kept on the computer and the data processing system is closed a day or two ahead of the monthly financial closing. This early closing allows the transfer of actual costs to users each month. As an example, this procedure has caused the divisions to reduce the size and cost of their data processing groups. In one division of this conglomerate, the data processing cash costs were reduced by almost 40 percent.

Data Processing as a Profit Center

An alternative method for controlling data processing is for data processing to bid for projects based upon its budget for the year and charge users accordingly. Data processing absorbs all costs that exceed the estimates and recognizes as income any excess in amounts transferred to users over actual costs. Therefore, any costs or credits remaining in data processing at year end measure the accuracy with which data processing estimated the costs of projects completed and in process. The danger with using this approach is that data processing may over-estimate the costs for every project to protect itself from absorbing any costs and to guarantee that it will show a profit! Remember, however, that potential competition from outside the firm limits this temptation.

> Firms which have adopted zero based budgeting have also benefited from the information provided about the costs of data processing. In one case, the method of processing projects was modified when the managers discovered that through additional programming they could reduce the costs of processing in the machine operations group and the reduction was greater than the costs of the additional programming.
>
> Another firm was spending too much money for maintenance programming relative to the results achieved. This firm reduced the costs of maintenance programming by approximately $10,000 per year, without any reduction in service, through increasing the productivity of its maintenance programmers.

Estimating the Cost of the Use of Data Processing Services Is Necessary

The projected total hours and dollars for running data processing for the next year should be estimated and accumulated by each data processing cost center. Each section of the data processing organization also estimates the amounts of its projected costs which are to be charged to users. The total to be spent in each section for the next year, when approved, is its operating objective or budget. From these estimates, which are separated into direct and indirect costs, hourly rates and overhead percentages are developed for charging costs to users for services rendered. Each section's estimated rates are used for pricing project requests and for bidding for data processing jobs within the firm. These bids are the input for users who will decide, on the basis of the bid, whether to use "in house" data processing services or choose another alternative.

> One data processing organization using this technique completely eliminated the use of outside data processing services because of its success in bidding for projects. This success reduced the corporation's cash outflow by approximately 10 percent.

Requests for Data Processing Services

Requests for data processing services originate with potential users and are submitted to the data processing division for action. Data processing replies by submitting a bid (cost estimate) for completing the work requested by the user. This could require preliminary investigation of the extent of the job by the data processing department. In addition, data processing can seek jobs by soliciting users and submitting proposals based upon the users' needs, i.e., data processing personnel in the course of their work might identify an application, review it with the user and submit a bid based upon their perception of its benefit to the user.

Generally, users are permitted to solicit bids from external sources as well. In these circumstances, however, proper consideration must be given to the effect of such a decision upon cash flow. It is possible that an outside service may underbid the internal data processing organization. However, if both estimates are compared strictly on the basis of the effect upon cash flow, it may be to the firm's disadvantage to purchase data processing services from outside. It is important that each alternative developed in response to a user's request be examined from the point of view of the effect it may have upon the discounted cash flow return to the firm.

> Fortunately, the data processing division of one large company was relatively small. The policy of the company was to compare bids from outside with those from internal sources based upon the total costs of each bid. Until the procedure was changed, it cost the company approximately $5,000 a year in additional cash outflow.

Following is an example of a zero budget report for a women's apparel manufacturer:

EXHIBIT 20

AN EXAMPLE OF A ZERO BUDGET FOR DATA PROCESSING (000)

Description[1]	19XX Budgeted[3] Amount	Amount[4] Charged To Users	Actual[5] Amounts Expended
Computer Operations			
Equipment Rental	$ 750.0	$ 800.0	$ 750.0
Operators Salaries	90.0	196.0	100.0
Overhead[2]	40.0		50.0
Total	$ 880.0	$ 996.0	$ 900.0
New Systems Programming			
Programmers Salaries	$ 100.0	$ 196.0	$ 120.0
Overhead[2]	50.0		50.0
Total	$ 150.0	$ 196.0	$ 170.0
Systems Analysts			
Analysts Salaries	$ 120.0	$ 256.0	$ 130.0
Overhead[2]	60.0		70.0
Total	$ 180.0	$ 256.0	$ 200.0
Operational Programming			
Programmers Salaries	$ 30.0		$ 30.0
Overhead[2]	15.0		20.0
Total	$ 45.0	N/A	$ 50.0
Maintenance Programming			
Programmers Salaries	$ 75.0	$ 176.0	$ 80.0
Overhead[2]	37.0		30.0
Total	$ 112.0	$ 176.0	$ 110.0
Planning and Equipment Evaluation			
Salaries	$ 40.0		$ 40.0
Support Costs[2]	15.0		20.0
Total	$ 55.0	N/A	$ 60.0

EXHIBIT 20 (Continued)

AN EXAMPLE OF A ZERO BUDGET FOR DATA PROCESSING (000)

Description[1]	19XX Budgeted[3] Amount	Amount[4] Charged To Users	Actual[5] Amounts Expended
Data Conversion			
Equipment Rental	$ 12.0	$ 15.0	$ 14.0
Salaries	45.0	126.0	60.0
Overhead[2]	25.0		30.0
Total	$ 82.0	$ 141.0	$ 104.0
Data Processing General Mgmt.			
Salaries	$ 120.0		$ 130.0
Support Costs[2]	60.0		75.0
Total	$ 180.0	N/A	$ 205.0
Grand Total	$1,684.0	$1,765.0	$1,799.0

[1]This schedule is a summary of a budget and a year's activity for a zero budgeted data processing operation in a manufacturing environment.

[2]For this illustration, fringe benefits costs are included in overhead and support costs rather than as part of labor costs. Also, overhead and support costs include purchases and/or rental of software and software packages.

[3]The budgeted amounts are also used as the basis for charging users. Users of data processing services are charged for actual hours used at the budgeted rates. Differences between amounts charged to users and actual costs are either absorbed by or accrue to data processing.

[4]In this case, the amounts charged to users of data processing services exceed budgeted amounts. This was caused by the use of more hours for projects than anticipated. The charges to users are allocated through direct departments and include overhead costs as well as costs for indirect departments. The excess charged ($81,000) would be a profit to data processing if the actual costs incurred did not exced the budget.

[5]The actual costs exceeded the budget by $115,000 and exceeded the amount charged to users by $34,000. Because the actual costs exceeded that charged to users, data processing must show a loss or an unfavorable variance from their zero budget. The unfavorable variance was caused by the use of more time than anticipated on projects and the attendant overtime and other costs.

Zero Budgeting in a Small Data Processing Service

An example of the successful use of zero budgeting is that of a data processing organization in a small financial firm in a consulting environment where bids are submitted to clients based upon the estimated number of hours of the central processing unit used for each client's work. All costs in the data processing section are related to the cost per hour for using the central processing unit.

The costs for the total organization, plus a profit, are estimated and accumulated and then divided by the total estimated central processing unit hours available. This rate is used to estimate jobs for clients and when multiplied by the actual CPU hours used is the basis for billing clients. Any differences between the actual costs and the billed costs are absorbed by the firm and either increase or reduce its profit.

Zero Based Budgeting in a Large Data Processing Organization

In this organization, the user has a choice of the services of data processing, the services of an outside service bureau, or the use of a manual system. If the user chooses to use the services of central data processing, the estimate of the cost of the project is the amount of cost agreed upon at the beginning for that project. The estimate includes the projected hours needed for the project multiplied by the estimated hourly rate for each section that must process the job. These estimates are adjusted to actual, quarterly or annually as requested by the user. In addition, some projects at the request of the user, are closed early in the month and the actual costs are available monthly. Most users, however, request adjustments at quarterly intervals and rely upon estimates monthly.

If, when the estimates are adjusted, the actual costs differ from the estimates by 5 percent or more, the question of who will absorb the difference is negotiated between data processing and the user. The user is not required to accept the charge for the amount by which the actual cost exceeds the estimate (if the excess is equal to 5 percent or more) and data processing can be forced to absorb the cost over-run. However, if the excess cost is caused by a change in the scope of the work required, and these changes in scope were initiated or agreed to by the user, the disposition of the excess is not subject to negotiation.

The amounts charged to users in this firm are accumulated by each section within data processing. In the computer operations section, users are charged on the basis of the number of central processing unit hours and operator hours required for each job. The charge is computed by multiplying actual hours required by the actual rates.

A percentage is added to the operator labor costs to cover the overhead (indirect costs) of the computer operations cost center. In addition, the percentage added to the operator labor costs includes an allocation for the costs of operational programming, the costs of planning and equipment evaluation, and an amount to cover the costs of data processing general management. The applicable percentages for these overhead costs are totaled within the data processing cost system. The billing to the user only has a consolidated percentage and all of the allocations are added together rather than listed separately.

In this data processing organization, new systems programming is charged to users based upon the hours used for each project multiplied by the actual labor rate for new systems programmers. In addition, a percentage is added which includes the costs of the overhead of the new systems programming section, and an allocation for the costs of data processing general management.

Systems analysis is allocated to users on the basis of the number of analyst hours required for each job multiplied by their actual pay rate including fringe benefits, plus a percentage of their labor cost. The percentage is added to cover the indirect costs of operating the systems analyst section, i.e., systems analyst managers, supplies, other expenses and facilities. Also, an amount is added to the percentage to recover the costs of data processing general management.

Operational programming is allocated to users as an add-on percentage to the computer operator labor costs charged to each project and thus to each user. This section is not separately identified for users. It is included as an overhead item in the computer operations cost center.

Maintenance programming is charged to users based upon the hours required to update and revise existing programs. The allocation includes actual rates for direct maintenance programming labor plus a percentage for indirect costs incurred in the operation of maintenance programming, including supervision, supplies, facilities costs, and a percentage for data processing general management.

Planning and equipment evaluation costs are allocated to users as a percentage of computer operator labor dollars. Therefore, these costs are not identified separately for users.

Data conversion costs are assigned to projects and thus to users, in two ways, depending upon whether the costs are for equipment or for labor. The costs of the data conversion equipment are assigned to projects by the number of data conversion equipment hours required for each project. The hours of machine use are multiplied by the rates of depreciation or rental costs for the equipment and these costs are transferred to the user's project. In addition, projects are charged for the direct labor costs of conversion based upon the hours required for each job multiplied by the rate for conversion direct labor. In addition, a percentage is added to data conversion direct labor for the overhead costs of the data conversion section, i.e., its managers, facilities costs, and supplies. Included, also, is a percentage for the cost of data processing general management absorbed by the data conversion section.

The costs of data processing general management are charged to users as a percentage of the direct labor dollars of computer operators, new systems programmers, systems analysts, maintenance programmers, and data conversion labor. Therefore, the costs of this section cannot be identified by users.

Summary

The zero based budgeting of data processing, despite the fact that it requires the use of a firm's resources to implement and maintain, is effective for controlling the costs and thus the growth and use of data processing. Zero based budgeting may appear to be a lengthy and costly process; however, it is easily cost justified. Its largest cost is its initial installation.

The direct advantage of zero based budgeting data processing is the more effective use of this resource. It will be applied to the more profitable and more important projects from the point of view of the whole firm. The result is that data processing is more productive and a higher return accrues to the firm.

Through effective use of data processing, the firm receives more productivity for its investment and profits are increased. Much has been written about the huge losses from, and the costs of, the misuse of data processing services, but it is estimated that the proper use of this resource through zero based budgeting can add as much as 5 percent to the firm's net income each fiscal year through increased productivity and the reduction of the operating costs of data processing. The estimated increase in net income is after deduction of the costs of the zero based budgeting system.

The use of zero based budgeting will not only increase the profits of the firm, but will enhance the stature and effectiveness of data processing within the firm. If more firms had used this technique, data processing might have been used more quickly and more effectively throughout the business community. The problems encountered in attempting to use data processing effectively are well known. Zero based budgeting is a very practical and useful solution.

Controlling the Costs of Maintenance Through Zero Based Budgeting

Inflation, energy costs, the costs of trade labor, and the lack of incentive to produce have pushed the costs of maintenance to a point where innovative changes are needed to keep these costs to a minimum and to maintain or increase productivity. Because maintenance is required in all parts of a firm, the costs of maintenance affect the total costs of the firm. If maintenance costs are unreasonable, other operating costs will be high!

The most effective method for controlling departmental costs is to place the responsibility for the level of the costs upon the department manager and measure his performance. If the maintenance manager is required to "sell" his services to users and recover his operating costs, responsibility and control are integrated at the management level where corrective action can be taken. The manager who incurs the maintenance costs must "sell" the services at a competitive price and quality.

With zero based budgeting the internal maintenance department must compete with maintenance services outside the firm. The user of maintenance services has a choice! He can choose the maintenance service which will cost him the least. The presence of competition will restrain the extravagance of the internal maintenance manager.

When normal maintenance service is needed the user has at least two options: (a) he can solicit bids from outside as well as from the inside maintenance department and select the lowest bid; or (b) he can, if the outside service is the lower bidder, discuss the bids with the in-house maintenance manager to reduce the in-house costs. The user may be able to convince the in-house maintenance department to do the work for the same price as the outsider. The user, by taking advantage of the competitive environment, can keep his maintenance costs to a minimum.

Zero based budgeting will have a number of positive effects upon the in-house maintenance department. It will force the maintenance manager to plan. The level of maintenance activity must be projected as well as the costs anticipated. It forces the maintenance manager to become aware of the nature and functions of costs. He will not only become familiar with the levels of costs, but he will become familiar with how costs relate to productivity. Zero based budgeting will educate the maintenance manager on the nature and control of costs.

One potential problem which must be resolved, if the maintenance department is zero based budgeted, is the cost of emergency maintenance. Fortunately, emergency maintenance is usually a small part of total maintenance costs. However, when an emergency occurs the repairs must be done quickly and the costs determined at some other time.

Treating the Maintenance Department as a Profit Center

Because the maintenance department must compete with outside maintenance services it can be allowed to return a profit similar to that earned by outside maintenance services. To treat the maintenance department as a profit center, the first step is to estimate the operating hours and costs for the coming fiscal year. For example:

PROJECTED OPERATING MAINTENANCE DEPARTMENT HOURS AND COSTS FOR FISCAL YEAR 19XX

Description	Hours	Amount
Electricians Salaries	5,000	$ 100,000
Carpenters Salaries	10,000	$ 200,000
Other Trade Salaries	10,000	$ 200,000
Clerical Salaries	4,000	$ 40,000
Supervisory Salaries	2,000	$ 60,000
Fringe Benefits	—	$ 180,000
Materials Needed	—	$ 300,000
Allocated Costs	—	$ 800,000
Total Estimated Hours and Costs	31,000	$1,880,000

The next step is to estimate the number of hours of maintenance which will be performed for users during the fiscal year. This can be estimated from history, from a review of the maintenance record of major equipment items, or from interviewing potential users. If, for example, it is estimated that 30,000 hours of maintenance will be performed for users during the fiscal year, it is easy to compute the billing rate per hour for maintenance performed. The billing rate is the total estimated cost of $1,880,000 divided by 30,000 hours which are the projected billing hours or approximately $63.00 per hour. However, if the maintenance department is to be treated as a profit center a profit factor must be added. Assuming an independent maintenance contractor would earn 10 percent profit per hour, the inside maintenance service, because of its unique position, is allowed 5 percent. The hourly rate, including the 5 percent profit, equals approximately $66.00 per hour.

Therefore, during the next fiscal year it is projected that the inside maintenance department will bill 30,000 hours at $66.00 per hour or a total of $1,980,000. If $1,880,000 of projected cost is deducted from the projected billings, the result equals a projected profit of $100,000.

This rate, including profit if the maintenance department is treated as a profit center, will be used to bid for maintenance jobs.

The maintenance foreman will estimate the number of hours each job will require and multiply the estimated hours by the projected rate. The product of the calculation is the bid for performance of that job.

If the user selects the inside maintenance department to perform the work, the bid, unless modified by agreement to meet competition from outside maintenance services, is the contract for performance of the maintenance services. Should the actual hours differ from the estimated hours or the actual costs vary from the estimated costs, the maintenance department must add or subtract the difference from its profit. The balance, if any, in the maintenance department cost center is the profit or loss or unallocated costs from performing inside maintenance services.

The actual costs incurred by the maintenance department are accumulated throughout the fiscal year and compared, at year end, to the projections and the amounts actually charged to users. An unfavorable comparison may cause a change in the bid rates and/or a restructuring of the costs of operating the inside maintenance department. If for example, 31,000 hours of maintenance was actually performed, the amount charged to users would equal $2,046,000. If it is assumed that the actual costs incurred by the maintenance department were $2,100,000, the department would show a net loss of $54,000 for the year ($2,100,000—$2,046,000).

This result indicates that the number of hours of maintenance to be performed were underestimated as was the maintenance cost per hour. The actual cost per hour was approximately $68.00 rather than $66.00 and that rate did not include a profit! With this performance, an investigation of the causes is necessary. The investigation may result in a cost reduction program for the maintenance department, a review of the estimating procedures used, or a restructuring of the maintenance department's operating methods.

The Role of the User

With zero based budgeting the user has a direct influence upon the costs and quality of maintenance. If management requires that costs be kept to a minimum, the maintenance department will be forced, from pressure from users, to keep costs as low as possible.

The user has a choice! He can choose between the inside and

outside services, and can compare the costs of each! The user can force the inside maintenance department to meet the bids from outside services!

If, however, the user is granted a choice between outside and inside maintenance services, the firm must be prepared to consider the effect of outside purchases upon cash flow. In the short run, a continual use of outside maintenance services plus supporting a maintenance department would use cash that the firm might need for other purposes. In the long run, however, the reduction in cash flow from reduced maintenance costs could more than offset the short-run cash outflow.

The user will need to make special arrangements for emergency jobs. Emergency jobs, which usually do not allow time for solicitation of bids must be treated separately. The alternatives for the user are: (a) to bear the costs of inside maintenance, regardless of the extent of those costs, or (b) use a standard cost for emergency work; or (c) use after-the-fact bidding to establish the costs.

Depending upon the benefit—cost relationship, i.e. the costs of downtime versus the costs of doing the maintenance, the user and the maintenance department could agree at the start of each fiscal year, on a standard rate to be applied to the actual hours of emergency maintenance. Or the maintenance department could set aside a standard number of hours at a standard rate for emergency work. Then a special arrangement would only be required if the emergency work exceeded the amount set aside. Another alternative is to solicit outside bids after the emergency work has been completed and to charge the user for the maintenance services accordingly!

Summary

The maintenance department is another example of the use of zero based budgeting for effective cost control. Zero based budgeting forces the inside maintenance department to compete with outside services if it is to remain intact.

For the firm, the benefits of zero based budgeting are a cost-conscious maintenance manager, less cost (and cash outflow) for maintenance services than is possible otherwise, and increased profits! Each dollar saved on the costs of maintenance adds a dollar to the firm's "bottom-line."

Chapter 8

Reporting on Marketing Programs

How to Tailor Reports on Marketing Programs to Maximize Product Profit Contribution

This chapter describes reporting techniques that will result in getting the most benefit from marketing programs. The reports are structured to emphasize the contribution of each product and program. The emphasis is on terms which are most important to the user — profit margin after variable costs, and contribution to fixed costs and profits. The need for quick reporting to support continuous adjustment of plans is highlighted. The chapter also suggests methods for adjusting a program as actual results are received and presents examples of selection of products from marketing reports and program reports.

Components for Effective Reporting on Marketing Programs and Plans

The unit variable manufacturing costs are needed for major products based principally upon actual cost experience, modified for anticipated improvements. For miscellaneous products included in the plan, a percentage estimate of variable manufacturing cost will suffice. For the major products, the unit price at each expected sales volume is multiplied by the quantity to compute the total estimated sales revenue.

The unit variable manufacturing cost is multiplied by the total quantity expected to be sold to arrive at the total variable manufacturing cost, which is deducted from the total revenue per product to arrive at the expected gross profit contribution of each major product in the program. The incremental selling costs for each major product and for the total program are deducted from the expected gross profit. The incremental selling costs include commissions to be paid to the salesmen and other incentives offered as part of the sales program. Usually, a comprehensive marketing program includes sales incentives which are related directly to the products included in the program. The objective is to tailor the sales incentives to that particular program.

The cost of a sales program would be incomplete without the inclusion of incremental point of sale incentives and other promotional expenses. Such promotional costs may include point of sale advertising such as display racks, posters, cards, etc., and salesmen incentives for distributors' or retailers' salesmen such as cash payments or the awarding of points which are convertible into cash based upon the number and type of products sold. Trade or cash discounts offered in the program must be explicitly identified. Usually, marketing programs will include incremental trade discounts which are larger than the usual trade discounts offered. The trade discounts are usually supplemented by cash discounts and credit terms which are specifically designed for that program. The cash discounts offered and the credit terms could be chosen from either side of a broad spectrum. The discounts could be small with very generous payment terms or the discounts could be very large with short payment periods.

These costs are totaled and deducted from the gross contribution margin of the program to determine the program's net contribution. It is necessary to identify this amount to evaluate the program and measure its contribution to earnings. At this point, the program contribution can be identified and measured by sales territory, by product line or by a number of other alternatives. The costs included in the program thus far can be traced to a particular salesman or sales territory or to a product line or group of products through a simple code. Through the code, the firm can compare the actual results achieved by specific and detailed parts of the organization to the program plan.

After computation of the net contribution by sub-parts of the organization, the cost of advertising for the program is deducted to arrive at the final contribution to profits from the marketing program. Advertising costs include radio, television, newspapers, circulars and fliers, and any other brochures which are not limited in circulation or coverage to a specific territory or point of sale. Advertising costs are more difficult to identify with and relate to a particular sale or to a particular part of the organization. However, the only advertising cost which can be charged to the marketing program is the incremental marketing cost.

Also included in the marketing program are the names and positions of the individuals responsible for the development of and execution of the program. Often the success of a program depends upon accountability, including the identification of the individuals responsible for development and execution of the program. There cannot be any doubt about responsibility for the program if it is to succeed.

> An extremely successful manufacturer of small appliances markets its consumer products through six-month marketing programs. While one program is being implemented, another program is being planned. Their successful marketing effort is dependent upon continuous programs. In addition, while a six-month marketing program is in progress, another short-range program may be implemented to solve a particular problem, such as the failure of the original program to meet its objectives. Regardless, however, of the number of programs in progress or the stage of completion of each program, every one is planned in detail and the results are measured against that plan. Each plan includes details from product price to point of sale displays, salesmen incentives, and all advertising. It is also a cardinal rule of this manufacturer that the individuals responsible for each program be identified. The results have been a minimum increase of 10% per annum in market share and a similar increase in before-tax net income.

Development of a Marketing Program

The development of a detailed marketing plan entails the comparison of, and choosing from, a number of alternative plans. Each plan is constructed independently with differing quantities, prices and, in some instances, products. To choose between the alternatives, the following characteristics of the plans are compared:

1. *Expected quantities to be sold*—the plans are compared to determine whether or not the market penetration sought is included. The quantities of each product to be sold in each plan are the measure of the market penetration. After the quantities of products which represent the desired market penetration are chosen, the quantities required are discussed with the manufacturing organization to minimize inventory levels and coordinate sales with the manufacturing schedule. The objectives of this discussion are to reduce excess inventories and to take advantage of manufacturing efficiences.

2. *Pricing*—each plan is reviewed to evaluate the prices for each product. The objective is to determine if the planned pricing strategy will increase share of market without spoiling the market price. In addition, the prices are reviewed to evaluate their reasonableness in relation to the quantity expected to be sold. The effect of the programs upon the share of market is a primary consideration when choosing between programs. The purpose of the plan is to take share of market from competitors which involves a cost, therefore, price reductions, advertising costs and other selling costs can be viewed as costs of gaining (or purchasing) market share. Through the plan, the attempt is made to gain as much of the share of market as possible with the least possible cost.

If there are any difficulties with the quantities of the products anticipated to be sold in any program being available, then the program should be either altered or scrapped. It is a waste to print point of sale material and advertise products which are not available.

3. An intangible but important factor to consider when choosing a marketing program is the *expected reaction of competitors.* If the proposed program emphasizes products in which competitors are also strong, it may be wise to modify the program, rather than support competitors' sales through the program's advertising. If the strategy is to attack competitors where they are strong, then the advertising costs must be carefully evaluated to maximize their competitive effect.

4. Another important factor to consider is the *general economic situation.* The influence of general economic conditions upon employ-

ment and income may be critical to the success of a marketing program. If the products included in the program are in the higher price ranges and the economy is on the downswing, it may be more prudent to cancel the program and substitute a program which emphasizes lower priced products.

After weighing the alternatives, the program which is choosen is the one which will accomplish the marketing objectives and earn the largest contribution to income. The final measure of success of a marketing program is its contributions to the bottom line. However, the contribution must be made while accomplishing the marketing objectives. Therefore, the two criteria for evaluating a marketing program are its ability to accomplish the marketing objectives and the amount of its contribution to profits.

> From a failure which cost the firm approximately 10 percent of its bottom line forecast for that fiscal year, one firm learned to make a closer evaluation of competitors' possible reactions in future marketing programs. The firm attempted to capture share of market and increase profits through a sales program which did not consider all the possible reactions of competitors. The products in the program were directly comparable to those of a competitor whose acceptance in the market was greater than this firm's. The result was the competitor reacted strongly and kept the firm from accomplishing its marketing and profit objectives. The firm's failure to recognize that it was attacking a competitor at its strongest point caused the marketing program to miss its objectives. When planning a marketing program the objective should be to capture a weak, not strong, market from a competitor.

The Benefits of Reporting upon Marketing Programs

Continual reporting on the progress of marketing programs results in the largest possible profit contribution per program. In addition, continuous reporting of results against plan creates a data bank of information about the demand conditions for various products within the program markets and of the strategies of competitors. The information is gathered from an analysis of the market's response to the prices, quantities and products included in the program. The reaction of competitors is another source of information about the market.

If a competitor does not react, it is possible the program was poorly planned and is a potential failure. On the other hand, if competitors react strongly, it could mean they have been caught unprepared or conversely that the program erroneously emphasizes products in which competitors have more market acceptance.

Another benefit of reporting is that it supports the continuous adjustment of the program to the most efficient balance between accomplishing the market objectives and maximizing the program's profit contribution. Through reporting results against plan, the necessary adjustments can be identified to redirect the program and reach the desired objectives.

To be effective, however, the reporting interval must be as short as possible. The ideal reporting period is weekly. If it is not possible to report weekly, reports should be prepared at least monthly. It can not be overemphasized that the shorter reporting interval results in faster feedback and more rapid adjustments to the program. The more rapidly necessary adjustments are made to the program, the larger the probability of maximum benefit.

The most effective tool to use for reporting on marketing programs is the computer. The computer's speed, accuracy and reasonable cost for processing large quantities of data make it ideal for this purpose.

> One Fortune 500 company computes, summarizes and prints the alternative marketing programs on the computer. The computer compares key items such as quantities, prices, share of market, and chooses the most favorable programs. This company also uses the computer to report actual results weekly, including the cumulative to date since the program started. Thus the firm knows within one week of the start of a program how it is progressing. Having the information this quickly allows the company to adjust product mix, prices, advertising, sales incentives, etc. This firm has continuously, for the past 15 years, taken share of market from its competitors and enjoyed the resulting increase in profits and cash flow.

If a computer is not available and only monthly reporting is possible, the monthly report should be distributed quickly even if it is necessary to include some estimates in the report. Even though monthly reporting is the least acceptable reporting period, it is better to adjust the program based upon monthly information than not to adjust it at all.

Reporting is necessary if adjustments are to be made in program pricing. The sales results may indicate a lack of market response to product prices or a failure to reach the profit objectives despite strong product sales. Through reporting, which has made this information available, a decision can be made whether, in the first case, to lower prices or, in the second, to increase them. The advertising investment can be modified early in the program. Again, these decisions must be correlated with the manufacturing schedule.

An analysis should be made of cash discounts to determine how many customers are taking advantage of the discount and whether the response is greatest for products with the largest cash and trade discounts. From the analysis, decisions can be made to increase or decrease the trade and cash discounts and get the program back on the profit track.

After examining the early reports, it may be decided to add other selling incentives to the program to increase profitability or to prevent a program from failing. Incentive prizes could be added or volume discounts increased. Despite monthly reporting, if that is the only reporting available, the marketing programs should be adjusted by actual results achieved as soon as possible.

> Successful firms have alternate plans for cash discounts, trade discounts and credit terms, for example, to use with each program. If the marketing program is not meeting its objectives with the assigned discounts and terms, another set is ready. This approach is particularly useful if the managers believe a minor change in the program is all that is required for it to meet its goals. Usually, a marketing program causes more enthusiasm and market response early in its life, therefore, quick feedback, analysis and execution will allow time to change to a second or third alternate credit and discount policy and save the program. Firms that use these methods are among the most profitable in their industries. Their profit premiums consistently range from 10 to 60 percent above those of their competitors.

Techniques for Reporting on Marketing Programs

If reporting on marketing programs is to be meaningful and useful, the program must be planned in detail. At the planning stage, it may seem tedious and time-consuming to prepare a detailed program, but to get the largest profit from a program, this work must be done at the beginning. The alternative is to forgo profits. The program must be started by marketing with a plan for each major product. Usually, major products are defined as those products which are expected to sell above a minimum quantity. Each major product is planned in detail, including the expected variations in sales during the life of the program. Often the sales of each major product are planned by week or month for the life of the program. This is the responsibility of the marketing department. The actual results are summarized similarly for accurate comparison with the plan. If the program and the results include the seasonability of the sales, the comparison is more useful. The more useful the comparison, the more probable that proper choices will be made to correct a faltering program.

The detailed report which compares the actual to the plan must include prices, quantities, product mix, sales incentives and advertising. The financial department should point out those areas of the program in which there are significant differences between the plan and the actual results. From that point, marketing and finance must investigate the causes of the deviations and recommend corrective action. During the investigation, certain questions will arise which require answers, such as: Were the quantities to be sold included in the plan overly optimistic at the planned price level? Were the prices included in the plan unobtainable?

An example of corrective action to salvage a failing plan is to increase or decrease the selling prices of the various products. The analysis of such a recommendation should compare the estimated quantities to be sold at each price for the effect upon revenue of the change in price and the resultant change in quantities sold. Will the change in quantities sold offset the loss of revenue from a price decrease and vice versa?

The managers must make this decision with one eye on the inventory levels of various products. Lowering price to increase quantities sold is useless unless there are enough products in inventory to accommodate the sales increase. If it is decided to build inventories, the cost of carrying the increase in inventories is an important consideration because it is chargeable to the program and affects its profit contribution. Judgment is necessary for deciding when to respond to a program's not meeting its objectives. If the information about the program's actual results is available within a week, the temptation is to react immediately. However, it may be that the market has not adjusted to the effects of the program and price differentials may not have been reacted to throughout the market. Also, the short-run reaction of competitors may not indicate their long-range policy. That policy will depend upon their market and financial strength as well as the inventories they have available and the flexibility of their manufacturing schedules.

Additionally, the effect of advertising is not immediate. There is usually a period of time over which advertising becomes effective. Therefore, choosing when to revise a program is a managerial/marketing decision requiring experience and judgment.

A very important part of a sales program is the product mix. Often the product mix is designed to meet market requirements, therefore, the failure of the mix is caused either by faulty design of the program or by a change in the market requirements. In either case, the total plan must be reviewed by marketing because of product inventory restrictions and advertising commitments.

A human problem may result if sales are concentrated in the lower price items of the program. It may mean the sales force is taking the road of least resistance and over-emphasizing the lower priced products. If this is the case, the sales incentives should be revised to redirect the salesmen's efforts. On the other hand, if the advertising effort has been misplaced, a decision should be made immediately to redirect the advertising effort. Advertising has a lag effect and will not change product sales immediately after it has been redirected. To insure the success of sales programs, the advertising must be carefully planned and committed as the plan progresses to prevent an "irreversible" over-commitment. In addition, the product emphasis of the point of sale incentives should be monitored. This is difficult to redirect because of the advance commitment.

Forecasting and Reporting on Marketing Programs as Cost Control Tools

Cost control implies knowledge of a level of cost at which costs are under control. A marketing program which includes the desired level of profit defines the level at which costs are under control. Reporting against the program causes the necessary reaction by managers to correct any unplanned level of costs or to adjust costs so they are compatible with the marketing results.

Evaluating marketing programs by the contribution margin means the deduction from gross sales of at least the following costs: (a) unit variable manufacturing costs, (b) extra discounts, both trade and cash, (c) the opportunity costs of extra payment days, (d) salesmen's incentives, (e) customer incentives, (f) point of sale promotional material and (g) advertising expenses. If the program is meeting its objectives, costs must be kept at or below the plan. If the program does not meet the sales objectives, the costs must be reduced accordingly.

The program includes objectives for each element of cost and the actual costs are analyzed weekly and cumulatively throughout the program. For example, the unit variable cost analysis has the following details:

ANALYSIS OF MANUFACTURING COSTS

Description	Plan	Actual	Variance
Direct Material	$ XXX	$ XXX	$ XXX
Direct Labor	XXX	XXX	XXX
Fringe Benefits	XXX	XXX	XXX
Other Direct Costs	XXX	XXX	XXX
Material Handlers	XXX	XXX	XXX
Oilers	XXX	XXX	XXX
Supplies	XXX	XXX	XXX
Other Indirect Costs	XXX	XXX	XXX
Total Variable Unit Costs	$ XXX	$ XXX	$ XXX

The non-manufacturing program costs are similarly analyzed. For example:

ANALYSIS OF PROGRAM NON-MANUFACTURING COSTS

Description	Actual	Plan	Variance
Discounts:			
Trade	$ XXX	$ XXX	$ XXX
Cash	$ XXX	$ XXX	$ XXX
Interest Forgone (Opportunity Cost)	$ XXX	$ XXX	$ XXX
Salesman Bonus	$ XXX	$ XXX	$ XXX
Customer Gifts	$ XXX	$ XXX	$ XXX
Display Material	$ XXX	$ XXX	$ XXX
Advertising	$ XXX	$ XXX	$ XXX
Total Non-Manufacturing Costs	$ XXX	$ XXX	$ XXX

Each cost element for each program is subject to the same analysis for meeting or improving upon the program's objectives. The analytical report will cause the firm's managers to react. New materials will be substituted for old and new methods found to lower unit manufacturing costs. If program prices are lower than expected, salesmen's incentives, point of sale displays, terms of sale, and advertising are reduced to the level required to maintain program profit margins. These cost analyses cause reactions which assure the firm of the profit margin it is seeking.

Using the Report as a Decision Tool

The effect of reporting upon marketing programs is to bring the need to choose to the attention of the firm's managers. The managers must not only decide whether to act or not but when to act. The report will emphasize where the problems are in the program, i.e., which products, and it must be kept in mind that the program has two objectives and all decisions must be in support of those objectives. Despite investigative work and recommendations from marketing and finance, the ultimate choice must be made by management. From the results reported, management may decide to abandon the total program. They may decide not to throw good money after bad. If it is decided to abandon the program, there should be a short-range program that can be inserted in its place. Planning for marketing programs must include as many alternatives as possible because of the importance of the marketing programs to the success of the firm.

The Marketing Program and the Computer

Because of the detailed planning required for marketing programs, a computer is the only tool to use. If a firm does not have computers of its own, there are other alternatives available. There is the possibility of buying time and space on someone else's computer. There are banks and other firms who lease time and space on their hardware. The difficulty with this approach is access to the computer when it is needed, security and the cost, which can be high.

Another possibility is the use of a time-sharing computer system. The basic data can be stored in the time-share computer for easy access. Special programs can be developed which apply to the stored data and the need for a complete and formal marketing program. Although this alternative is costly, it does provide immediate and simple access. In addition, the security is adequate. All costs for computer services are a cost of the marketing program.

> A major manufacturer with a better-than-average growth in profits over the last 20 years plans, modifies, and tracks its marketing programs weekly during their six-month life. Each expense category is analyzed each week for possible revision as the actual results are received. Included in the analysis are the type of product, the quantity of each product sold, the product pricing, the sales incentives used, the salesmen's commissions, the credit terms, the trade discounts and the advertising program. In each case, a marketing manager is assigned responsibility for the program and with help from the financial department analyzes the reports thoroughly and quickly. Changes are initiated when a program is failing to meet its objectives. The marketing staff reacts with decisiveness and speed. There is no doubt that the reason this manufacturer is the leader in its industry is because of the attention and effort it invests in its marketing programs. There is no profit without a sale. This manufacturer guarantees itself the sales, that the marketing objectives are met, and that the contribution to profit is as or better than planned. Because of this approach, this manufacturer has the largest share of market in its industry and increases its share each year. In addition, this firm is the most profitable in its field and earns at least a 10 percent annual profit premium over its competitors.

Example of a Six-Month Marketing Program for a Manufacturer of Consumer Products

This example consists of three ten-product marketing programs which were developed for comparison. The program which more closely meets the firm's objectives will be chosen for execution. After the most desirable program has been chosen and initiated, the actual results are compared to the program plan.

The example illustrates the detail required to build and report on a marketing program. The detail needed includes product quantities, prices, gross profit contribution, advertising, salesmen's incentives, point of sale incentives, trade discounts, functional discounts, cash discounts and credit terms. Three detailed programs from which the final marketing program was selected were constructed for comparison. None of the three programs was selected in total, but parts of each were included in the final selection. The selection criteria were profit contribution and the support of the marketing objectives such as taking share of market, support of other products in the program, effective use of advertising, and expected reactions of competitors. The three programs are the result of the analysis and comparison of at least four product alternatives for each product included in a program.

Reporting the final program selected and the expected results is only the beginning of the reporting process. From this point forward, the actual costs each week and month are reported column by column against program D (the program selected). Each report results in action by a manager to protect or improve the results that are included in the original plan.

EXHIBIT 21

DEVELOPMENT OF A MARKETING PROGRAM FOR A HARDGOODS MANUFACTURER

Product Code	Description	Unit* Sales Price	Quantity	Gross Sales	Trade Discount	Net Sales	Variable Mfg. Cost	Gross Profit
Program A								
#1	Hand Tool A	$10.00	10,000	$ 100.0	$ 10.0	$ 90.0	$ 50.0	$ 40.0
2	Power Tool A	19.00	40,000	760.0	76.0	684.0	360.0	324.0
3	Power Tool B	21.00	20,000	420.0	21.0	399.0	200.9	199.0
4	Power Tool C	20.00	22,000	440.0	44.0	396.0	220.0	176.0
5	Power Tool D	18.00	50,000	900.0	135.0	765.0	450.0	315.0
6	Power Tool E	17.00	60,000	1,020.0	102.0	918.0	480.0	438.0
7	Power Tool F	16.00	70,000	1,120.0	224.0	896.0	560.0	336.0
8	Power Tool G	11.00	100,000	1,100.0	165.0	935.0	500.0	435.0
9	Power Tool H	13.00	90,000	1,170.0	234.0	936.0	540.0	396.0
10	Power Tool I	50.00	5,000	250.0	25.0	225.0	115.0	110.0
	Total			$7,280.0	$1,036.0	$6,244.0	$3,475.0	$2,769.0

*These prices are illustrative only. Usually, for marketing reasons, prices are expressed as $9.95, or $49.99, or $19.95.

Product Code	Description	Unit* Sales Price	Quantity	Gross Sales	Trade Discount	Net Sales	Variable Mfg. Cost	Gross Profit
Program B								
#1	Hand Tool A	$ 9.00	14,000	$ 126.0	$ 13.0	$ 113.0	$ 63.0	$ 50.0
2	Power Tool A	18.00	49,000	882.0	88.0	794.0	421.0	373.0
3	Power Tool B	19.00	24,000	456.0	23.0	433.0	218.0	215.0
4	Power Tool C	19.00	25,000	475.0	48.0	427.0	238.0	189.0
5	Power Tool D	20.00	40,000	800.0	120.0	680.0	400.0	280.0
6	Power Tool E	17.00	60,000	1,020.0	102.0	918.0	480.0	438.0
7	Power Tool F	21.00	50,000	1,050.0	210.0	840.0	525.0	315.0
8	Power Tool G	12.00	95,000	1,140.0	171.0	969.0	520.0	449.0
9	Power Tool H	15.00	75,000	1,125.0	225.0	900.0	518.0	382.0
10	Power Tool I	50.00	6,000	300.0	30.0	270.0	140.0	130.0
	Total			$7,374.0	$1,030.0	$6,344.0	$3,523.0	$2,821.0

*The prices and quantities included in this program were derived from marketing estimates of the quantities which would be sold at the prices included in this program. The prices like those in Program A, are illustrative only.

EXHIBIT 21 — Development of a Marketing Program — Hardgoods Manufacturer (Continued)

Product Code	Description	Advertising And Point Of Sale Inc.	Mfg. Salesmen's Incentives	Wholesale Salesmen Incentive	Est. Costs Cash Disc. & Credit Terms**	Net Program Contribution	Contribution % of Net Sales
Program A (Cont'd)							
#1	Hand Tool A	$ 10.0	$ 9.0	$ 5.0	$ 4.0	$ 12.0	13.3%
2	Power Tool A	80.0	68.0	34.0	27.0	115.0	16.8
3	Power Tool B	20.0	40.0	20.0	16.0	103.0	25.8
4	Power Tool C	22.0	40.0	20.0	16.0	78.0	19.7
5	Power Tool D	100.9	77.0	38.0	31.0	69.0	9.0
6	Power Tool E	120.0	92.0	46.0	37.0	143.0	15.6
7	Power Tool F	140.0	90.0	45.0	36.0	25.0	2.8
8	Power Tool G	200.0	94.0	47.0	37.0	57.0	6.1
9	Power Tool H	180.0	94.0	47.0	37.0	38.0	4.1
10	Power Tool I	5.0	23.0	10.0	9.0	63.0	28.0
	Total	$877.0	$627.0	$312.0	$250.0	$703.0	11.3%
Program B (Cont'd)							
#1	Hand Tool A	$ 14.0	11.0	$ 6.0	$ 5.0	$ 14.0	12.4%
2	Power Tool A	98.0	79.0	39.0	32.0	125.0	15.7
3	Power Tool B	24.0	43.0	22.0	17.0	109.0	25.2
4	Power Tool C	25.0	43.0	22.0	17.0	82.0	19.2
5	Power Tool D	80.0	68.0	34.0	27.0	71.0	10.4
6	Power Tool E	120.0	92.0	46.0	37.0	143.0	15.6
7	Power Tool F	100.0	84.0	42.9	34.0	55.0	6.5
8	Power Tool G	190.0	97.0	49.0	39.0	74.0	7.6
9	Power Tool H	150.0	90.0	45.0	36.0	61.0	6.8
10	Power Tool I	12.0	27.0	13.0	11.0	67.0	24.8
	Total	$813.0	$634.0	$318.0	$255.0	$801.0	12.6%

**The cash discount offered is 3% for payment within 10 days of invoice date or Net 180 days (6 months.) It is estimated that ½ the net sales will be at the 3% discount and ½ at net 180 days which cost ½ year's interest at an effective interest rate of 10% per annum (rounded to thousands of dollars).

The estimated costs of the cash discount and credit terms are computed the same way for each program.

EXHIBIT 21 (continued)

DEVELOPMENT OF A MARKETING PROGRAM FOR A HARDGOODS MANUFACTURER

Product Code	Description	Unit* Sales Price	Estimated Quantity	Gross Sales	Trade Discount	Net Sales	Variable Mfg. Cost	Gross Profit
Program C								
#1	Hand Tool A	$ 7.00	18,000	$ 126.0	$ 13.0	$ 113.0	$ 63.0	$ 50.0
2	Power Tool A	14.00	85,000	1,190.0	119.0	1,071.0	564.0	507.0
3	Power Tool B	18.00	25,000	450.0	23.0	427.0	214.0	213.0
4	Hand Tool C	21.00	20,000	420.0	42.0	378.0	210.0	168.0
5	Power Tool D	22.00	25,000	550.0	83.0	467.9	275.0	192.0
6	Power Tool E	17.00	60,000	1,020.0	102.0	918.0	480.0	438.0
7	Power Tool J	6.00	200,000	1,200.0	120.0	1,080.0	600.0	480.0
8	Power Tool K	7.00	170,000	1,190.0	119.0	1,071.0	595.0	476.0
9	Power Tool L	9.00	140,000	1,260.0	126.0	1,134.0	630.0	504.0
10	Power Tool I	100.00	2,000	200.0	20.0	180.0	92.0	88.0
	Total			$7,606.0	$767.0	$6,839.0	$3,723.0	$3,723.0

*The prices and quantities included in this program were derived from the marketing estimates of the quantities which would be sold at the prices included in the program. The prices, like those in programs A and B, are illustrative only.

The following program is the program selected for the six-month sales period. The program was selected by attempting to maximize the total dollar net program contribution without significantly diluting the percent contribution. However, some products were kept in the program because of the need to reduce inventory and one product was included because marketing believed the program would be incomplete without that product and it would have an adverse effect upon the sales of the remaining products to exclude it.

EXHIBIT 21 (continued)

DEVELOPMENT OF A MARKETING PROGRAM FOR A HARDGOODS MANUFACTURER

Product Code	Description	Advertising And Point of Sale Inc.	Mfg. Salesmen's Incentives	Wholesale Salesmen's Incentives	Est. Costs Cash Disc. & Credit Terms**	Net Program Contribution	Contribution % of Net Sales
Program C (Cont'd)							
#1	Hand Tool A	$ 18.0	$ 11.0	$ 6.0	$ 5.0	$ 10.0	8.8%
2	Power Tool A	170.0	107.0	53.0	43.0	134.0	12.5
3	Power Tool B	25.0	43.0	21.0	17.0	107.0	25.1
4	Power Tool C	20.0	38.0	19.0	15.0	76.0	20.0
5	Power Tool D	50.0	47.0	23.0	19.0	53.0	11.3
5	Power Tool E	120.0	92.0	41.0	37.0	148.0	16.1
7	Power Tool J	200.0	108.0	54.0	43.0	75.0	6.9
8	Power Tool K	170.0	107.0	53.0	43.0	103.0	9.6
9	Power Tool L	140.0	113.0	56.0	45.0	150.0	13.2
10	Power Tool I	2.0	18.0	9.0	7.0	25.0	28.8
	Total	$915.0	$684.0	$335.0	$274.0	$908.0	13.3%

**The estimated costs of the cash discount and credit terms are computed the same way for each marketing program.

EXHIBIT 21 (continued)

DEVELOPMENT OF A MARKETING PROGRAM FOR A HARDGOODS MANUFACTURER

Product Code	Description	Unit* Sales Price	Estimated Quantity	Gross Sales	Trade Discount	Net Sales	Variable Mfg. Cost	Gross Profit
Program D (The program selected)								
#1	Hand Tool A***	$ 9.00	14,000	$ 126.0	$ 13.0	$ 113.0	$ 63.0	$ 50.0
2	Power Tool A	14.00	85,000	1,190.0	119.0	1,071.0	564.0	507.0
3	Power Tool B	19.00	24,000	456.0	23.0	433.0	218.0	215.0
4	Power Tool C	19.00	25,000	475.0	48.0	427.0	238.0	189.0
5	Power Tool E***	17.00	60,000	1,020.0	102.0	918.0	480.0	438.0
6	Power Tool G	12.00	95,000	1,140.0	171.0	969.0	520.0	449.0
7	Power Tool J***	6.00	200,000	1,200.0	120.0	1,080.0	600.0	480.0
8	Power Tool K	7.00	170,000	1,190.0	119.0	1,071.0	595.0	476.0
9	Power Tool L	9.00	140,000	1,260.0	126.0	1,134.0	630.0	504.0
10	Power Tool I****	50.00	6,000	300.0	30.0	270.0	140.0	130.0
	Total			$8,357.0	$871.0	$7,486.0	$4,048.0	$3,438.0

*The prices and quantities included in this program were derived from marketing estimates of the quantities which would be sold at the prices included in the program. The prices used for this program are, like those in programs A, B, and C, illustrative only.

**The estimated costs of the cash discounts and credit terms are computed by the same method for each program.

***These products are included in the program because of the need to reduce the quantities in inventory.

****This product is included in the program because of its effect upon the sales of the remainder of the products. If this product were excluded, the tool line offered in the program would be incomplete and the unit sales of all the tools in the program would be less.

EXHIBIT 21 (continued)

DEVELOPMENT OF A MARKETING PROGRAM FOR A HARDGOODS MANUFACTURER

Product Code	Description	Advertising And Point of Sale Inc.	Mfg. Salesmen's Incentives	Wholesale Salesmen's Incentives	Est. Costs Cash Disc. & Credit Terms**	Net Program Contribution	Contribution % of Net Sales
Program D (Cont'd)							
#1	Hand Tool A	$ 14.0	$ 11.0	$ 6.0	$ 5.0	$ 14.0	12.4%
2	Power Tool A	170.0	107.0	53.0	43.0	134.0	12.5
3	Power Tool B	24.0	43.0	22.0	17.0	109.0	25.2
4	Power Tool C	25.0	43.0	22.0	17.0	82.0	19.2
5	Power Tool E	120.0	92.0	46.0	37.0	143.0	15.6
6	Power Tool G	190.0	97.0	49.0	39.0	74.0	7.6
7	Power Tool J	200.0	108.0	54.0	43.0	75.0	6.0
8	Power Tool K	170.0	107.0	53.0	43.0	103.0	9.6
9	Power Tool L	140.0	113.0	56.0	45.0	150.0	13.2
10	Power Tool I	12.0	27.0	13.0	11.0	67.0	24.8
	Total	$1,065.0	$748.0	$374.0	$300.0	$951.0	12.7%

Chapter 9

Controlling Research and Development Costs for Profit

The Percent of Sales Approach to Research and Development Is Not Control

Often, because of the lack of an alternative, a firm's managers will choose the amount of resources to be invested in research and development by allocating a percentage of expected sales for research and development. The percentage applied is usually developed from the historical relationship between the firm's sales and research and development. If the historical relationship between research and development and the firm's sales is unclear or inconclusive, the managers will turn to a source outside the firm. They might use a percentage furnished by a trade association or published in industry data. There are also many publications in which the authors recommend a percentage relationship. When the managers of a firm cannot agree on the amount of funds to invest in research and development, and internal information is not useful, they will search for other alternatives.

Choosing the amount to be spent through this relationship does not result in controlling the costs of research and development. One of the most important elements for deciding between investment alternatives is the comparison of benefits to costs. The percentage of sales technique does not include a direct comparison of benefits and costs.

Controlling research and development is more complicated, but more effective. The most effective method for controlling research and development expenditures is a benefit and cost project by project analysis.

The Benefits from Controlling Research and Development

The adequate control of research and development costs results in increased market share, in growth, and greater profit. In the past, control of research and development has been informal and often lacking. Research and development was viewed as a mystic function which controlled itself. By reporting on these vital costs and using the reports for effective control, managers can focus the efforts of research and development on introducing better and less expensive products, and ahead of their competitors.

Effective Reporting Can Prevent Costly Missed Schedules

Research and development reports cannot be mere summaries of costs by projects and cost categories. To be effective they must emphasize the cost of delays in meeting schedules and costs of missing project budgets. The report on research and development should include the estimated costs of missed schedules or, conversely, the benefits resulting from early completion of a project. One reporting technique for approximating the cost of a missed project schedule is to multiply the estimated lost sales by the average gross margin percentage on the product to which the project is related. Because lost sales usually cannot be recaptured, the contribution from that project to profit and discretionary costs is lost.

This reporting technique forces management to consider the cost of a missed schedule when deciding upon the allocation of the resources included in research and development. The result is an emphasis by management on those projects which are missing their schedules and causing lost profits. This usually results in the rescheduling of projects and the meeting of, or improving upon, completion dates and the beating of competitors to the market. The effect of being first is to increase both market share and profits.

Computing the Value of Lost Sales

Lost sales can be computed from the financial analysis which was approved before the research and development work was undertaken. The gross margin on sales by period is included in the analysis and can be easily extracted. However, this technique is applicable to projects only when the total estimated research and development costs are not to be increased because of the failure to meet the schedule. This is a useful technique when the only variable which has been materially affected by the slippage is the scheduled completion date.

For example, schedules can be missed because of: (a) a backlog in the test department or other key department; (b) a delay in interpreting or reporting test results; (c) the delay of a project for one with a higher priority; or (d) because of lack of equipment or equipment failure. Because this report emphasizes the cost of the delay and brings that cost to the attention of the managers who can act upon that information, it is more valuable than the typical reporting on research and development! The desire to minimize the gross margin on sales lost because of a missed schedule causes research and development personnel to make every effort to develop and meet realistic schedules. The results for the firm are new and re-designed products which reach the market before competitors. When a project not only is delayed, but will also require more research and development hours than anticipated, a different method of computing the estimated cost is necessary.

Reporting When Research and Development Costs Will Exceed Plan

There are many reasons why there are variances from estimates of research and development hours required for projects. The scope of the work could have been underestimated, unforeseen problems may have been encountered in the development cycle, a cycle might have been added, or the failure of the project output to meet the test specifications caused further design, construction and testing work.

The estimated loss from a missed projection of research hours is the gross margin which would be earned on the lost sales plus the additional cost of research and development work required. The additional hours required from each group in research and development multiplied by the estimated direct hourly cost for each group equals the cost of the additional development work. The total of these calculations are the estimated additional costs for the delay.

Through the use of the total of the lost gross margin on sales and the added research and development costs, the effect upon the firm is brought to the attention of management. Unlike other reporting methods, this method quantifies the problem of missed objectives and leaves an impression upon the reader. The benefits to the firm are the introduction of less costly products on a more timely basis than competitors'.

What the Reports Must Include

To be effective, the reports must include the details of the costs of research and development. Research engineering is usually involved in basic research and is a primary part of research and development. It may or may not be directed toward an immediate benefit for the firm. This section of research and development could be engaged in long-range research into a new product or searching for new materials and methods to produce present products.

However, for each project undertaken by research engineering, an objective must be set. The objective includes dollar goals and a time of completion. The dollar amounts are what is expected to be spent on the project. The time factor is the estimated date when research engineering expects to complete the project. If these objectives are long-range, they can be disaggregated into fiscal year segments to correspond to the firm's financial records. The financial report will measure progress against these objectives.

The Research Engineering Department

Usually, in a research department there are a number of skills, such as scientists and engineers, technicians who support them, outside consultants, and secretarial or clerical support. To report accurately, information must be collected from all these sources.

The basic method for reporting is a job card which contains the project number and the hours spent on each project in addition to the usual payroll information. To avoid excessive clerical work, this can be subject to a limit, such as not reporting less than one hour against any project. The time spent which is not charged to a project, such as vacation, holiday and unaccounted-for time, is collected in an overhead account and spread over all of the projects upon which research engineering works. In addition to the financial report, the engineer or scientist in charge of the project must submit at each financial closing, usually monthly, a report of the physical percentage of completion of the project for comparison with the computed financial completion.

The scientists and engineers, as well as the technicians who work closely with the scientists and engineers, must complete job tickets for each project worked upon. These tickets are processed and the hours and amounts used against each project are recorded and reported by each group within research engineering.

The clerical and secretarial support for research engineering is usually charged to overhead accounts. However, if a project requires excessive effort by the clerical or secretarial staff, they can, by use of an exception job card, charge their time directly to a project. An acceptable rule for the cut-off is if it requires four hours or more of a clerk's or secretary's time, it should be charged directly to that project.

The manager of the research engineering section should also be charged to an overhead account and spread over all the projects. The overhead costs are spread over the projects each month by the percentage relationship of the overhead costs to the research engineering labor costs charged directly to each project. For a more accurate allocation of overhead, the labor and overhead should be accumulated through the fiscal year and the relationship established on a cumulative basis.

Particularly in a research environment, consultants may be hired to solve problems encountered in a project or group of projects. When the consultant submits his invoice, it should be charged, through the voucher register, to the project or projects for which the consultant was hired. Any other costs incurred by research engineering should be charged to overhead and spread over all the projects processed during that period. This is the only way to ensure reasonably accurate reporting.

> One firm in a very competitive environment expended large amounts for basic research. The research usually resulted in new products which kept the firm ahead of its competitors. Ideas for research projects usually originated from research engineers, development engineers, application engineers, or marketing specialists. The effort used for research kept that company's profits 10 to 15 percent per year greater than its nearest competition. This firm's share of market has increased continuously for 15 years. It reports on research and development weekly. Close monitoring is the reason its R & D is so successful!

Development Engineering

Development engineering begins where research engineering ends. This includes further development of current technology and the application of research advances to the current product line. The result can be a new product or new parts for current products which do the job better, because of the materials developed in the research department.

Each project in the development engineering department must have a dollar and time limit. The financial report measures the dollars spent and to be spent against the money objective, and the estimated completion data and the relative financial completion.

Generally, a development engineering department includes design engineers and scientists, draftsmen, test engineers and scientists, an experimental machine shop, statistical support, and administration. Each project introduced into development engineering must contain a detailed description of the work to be done and the source of the project. In addition, the narrative must specify the area or areas in the development department where the project will be introduced.

For each project, an estimated completion date and the estimated costs to be expended are computed by each group within developmental engineering. The total project costs are also listed by cost categories, such as labor and materials. The narrative, the completion date, and the projected costs are usually prepared by the originator of the project with the help of the managers and senior employees of the development groups affected.

The estimated costs and completion date are used to measure the progress of the project. The estimated completion date should be broken into segments relating to each development department. The breakdown facilitates a comparison of the schedule or plan with the progress of the project through each section of development. The exact point of breakdown or delay in the schedule can be identified and the causes researched.

The schedule is planned by consultation between the originator of the project, a representative of the marketing department, a representative of the chief of the development department, and members of each section of development. This same group should review any breakdowns between the schedule and the progress achieved. The schedule or plan is incorporated within the report issued by the financial department along with the actual progress. The actual progress is reported, at least monthly, to the financial department by each section of development engineering for inclusion in the financial report.

How to Establish Cost Objectives

The originator of the project, the financial department, and representatives of each section of development participate in establishing the cost objectives of the project. The cost estimate must include the direct costs for design engineers, draftsmen, test engineers, direct shop costs such as the experimental machine shop, and the indirect costs usually applied as a percentage of each group's direct costs which include support salaries, travel expenses, fringe benefits, and depreciation expense. Examples of groups which are classified as indirect are statistical support groups such as duplicating, secretaries, and engineering development managers.

Once the cost objective or budget has been established, the actual costs can be compared to it monthly or weekly to monitor the results against the plan. After the monthly (or weekly) report is issued, any material variance between the actual and planned or budgeted costs should be reviewed by the same group that established the objectives.

The cost goals may have been established mechanically by the project originator and the development engineer through estimating the hours and type of labor to be used on the project, including any of various specialties within research and development such as the test area or the experimental machine shop. The project number which is assigned by the financial department is the key number for matching the budgeted to the actual costs and hours for each group within development engineering.

The number assigned is usually consecutive by project, with groupings of meaningful data assigned special digits within the project number. For example, the last three digits of the number assigned may be consecutive for number of projects each year or since inception of the system. The first digit can represent the project's relationship to the firm's product line, such as a number which indicates the product is classified as a professional product, etc. The digits in the middle can be reserved for the department number and type of work; e.g., design, construction, test or prototype manufacture. However, regardless of the particular meaning assigned to the components of the project number, the project numbering method must be used consistently throughout research and development over a long period of time if data useful for managing that function is to be accumulated.

Illustrations

Three sample research and development reports are included in this chapter to illustrate the different approaches to reporting on research and development. These reports contain all the necessary information for measuring the success of a project and to alert management to any problems encountered in the engineering and development cycle. Unlike most reports, the reports selected emphasize who is responsible for the project and the extent to which the work has been completed physically, compared to the percent of the total cost incurred at the date of the report. More importantly, the reports emphasize the costs to the firm of missed schedules, which indicate to managers where the firm will benefit most from deploying resources or shifting the emphasis of research and development.

Exhibit 22 is an example of a research and development report for an equipment manufacturer. The report layout includes: (1) a brief description of the project — the description must be informative without disclosing any confidential information; (2) the project number; (3) the name of the manager of the project; (4) the project start and estimated completion dates; (5) the name of each group in research and development which will work on the project; (6) the estimated hours and costs to be incurred by each group working on the project; (7) the estimated percentage of physical completion and the cost percentage of completion for each project; (8) the actual cost to date; (9) the projected total hours for completion of the project; (10) the projected cost of the project at completion; and (11) the revised project completion date.

The benefits from this report are: (1) it fixes responsibility for meeting the project objectives; (2) it causes projects to be completed on time because of the visibility of missed schedules; and (3) projects are completed within the cost objectives because deviations become visible immediately for corrective action. The results for the firm are low cost products introduced on schedule which are ahead of the competition.

In this exhibit, drafting hours are included within the hours reported for design engineering, and in each case the projects are substantially "on target." Deviations from plan are not significant enough to cause special reporting or plan revisions.

This example is from the cumulative section of a monthly report. However, this report can be issued weekly, semi-monthly, or at almost any interval desired. A report similar to this is issued weekly in an abbreviated form. The more frequently it is issued, the quicker corrective action, if needed, can be taken and the more valuable the report. This report also has the advantage of being almost universally useful in any industry.

This exhibit is based upon the experience of a firm which treats research and development as a scarce resource and continuously monitors its performance. Because of its report-

EXHIBIT 22

RESEARCH AND DEVELOPMENT REPORT
From 1/1/xx thru 6/1/xx

Project Description	Project Manager	Project Number	Project Start Date	Est. Compl. Date	R & D Group	Est. Hours	Est. Cost
Redesign of product A to increase product life	Martin Matovcik	100111	5/ 1/x1	8/ 1/x1	Design Engr.	100	$ 1,000
			7/15/x1	9/15/x1	Constr. Engr.	30	1,500
			7/25/x1	9/15/x1	Exper. Mach. Shop	200	1,600
			9/20/x1	11/ 1/x1	Test. Engr.	500	10,000
			11/ 1/x1	11/15/x1	Release	40	400
	Project Total		5/ 1/x1	11/15/x1		870	$14,500
Development of Product B, a new product, to compete with Z Co.'s Product F	Gary Quill	100122	3/ 1/x1	1/ 1/x2	Design Engr.	2000	$20,000
			1/ 1/x2	4/ 1/x2	Constr. Engr.	1000	50,000
			4/ 1/x2	6/ 1/x2	Exper. Mach. Shop	500	4,000
			5/ 1/x2	11/ 1/x2	Test. Engr.	2000	40,000
			11/ 1/x2	1/ 1/x3	Release	50	500
	Project Total		3/ 1/x1	1/ 1/x3		5550	$114,500
Cost reduction· partial redesign of Product D to reduce its manufacturing cost	Terry Koontz	100131	2/ 1/x1	3/ 1/x1	Design Engr.	300	$ 3,000
			2/15/x1	4/15/x1	Constr. Engr.	100	5,000
			4/ 1/x1	5/ 1/x1	Exper. Mach. Shop	50	400
			5/ 1/x1	7/ 1/x1	Test. Engr.	400	8,000
			7/ 1/x1	7/15/x1	Release	20	200
	Project Total		2/ 1/x1	7/15/x1		870	$16,600

EXHIBIT 22 (continued)

RESEARCH AND DEVELOPMENT REPORT
From 1/1/xx thru 6/1/xx

Project Number	R & D Group	% Completion Cost	% Completion Phys.	Actual Cost To Date	Projected Total Hrs. For Compl.	Proj. Cost At Completion	Project Completion Date
100111	Design Engr.	10%	9%	$ 100	100	$ 1,000	8/ 1/x1
	Constr. Engr.	—	—	—	30	1,500	9/15/x1
	Exper. Mach. Shop	—	—	—	200	1,600	9/15/x1
	Test Engr.	—	—	—	500	10,000	11/ 1/x1
	Release	—	—	—	40	400	11/15/x1
Project Total		0.7%	0.7%	$ 100	870	$ 14,500	11/15/x1
100122	Design Engr.	100%	100%	$19,500	1,800	$ 19,500	1/ 1/x2
	Constr. Engr.	100%	100%	48,000	1,000	48,000	4/ 1/x2
	Exper. Mach. Shop	100%	100%	4,000	500	4,000	6/ 1/x2
	Test Engr.	20%	20%	8,000	2,000	40,000	11/ 1/x2
	Release	—	—	—	50	500	1/ 1/x3
Project Total		71%	71%	$79,500	5,350	$112,000	1/ 1/x3
100131	Design Engr.	100%	100%	$ 3,000	300	$ 3,000	3/ 1/x1
	Constr. Engr.	100%	100%	5,000	100	5,000	4/15/x1
	Exper. Mach. Shop	100%	100%	400	50	400	5/ 1/x1
	Test Engr.	50%	50%	4,000	400	8,000	7/ 1/x1
	Release	—	—	—	20	200	7/15/x1
Project Total		74.7%	75.0%	$12,400	870	$ 16,600	7/15/x1

ing technique and the resultant control it has over research and development, this firm leads its industry in profitable product redesigns and successful new product introductions. This has, in turn, caused this firm to lead its industry in profitability. Without reporting and the resultant control over the performance of research and development, this firm could not be the industry leader.

Exhibit 23 is an example of the computation of excess costs caused by the failure to meet the projected completion dates for the project. Project A includes the excess costs caused by the failure to meet the estimated completion date even though no additional monies are to be spent on the project. The excess costs result from the sales lost because of the delay. Project B, on the other hand, illustrates the additional costs caused by the failure to meet the expected completion date and the need for additional effort by research and development.

To be effective, this report must include: (1) the name of the responsible manager; (2) a brief project description; (3) the project number; (4) the project start and estimated completion dates; (5) the group designations that will work on the project; (6) the projected hours and costs to be incurred by each group; (7) the percentages of cost and physical completion of each project by group; (8) actual costs to the date of the report; (9) the projected hours and cost at completion; (10) the estimated completion date as of this report; and (11) the cost deviation and its composition caused by a delay in the completion date and/or the need for more research and development effort.

The firm benefits from the report because the costs of deviations from objectives are identified, causing: (1) project costs to be met; (2) schedules to be adhered to; and (3) planning to be done more carefully to avoid unexpected expenditures on research and development.

As in Exhibit 22 drafting hours are included in design engineering. The values included as the costs of schedule deviations were computed with the participation of the research and development group. Therefore, the deviation values are, after any safety factors, included in the original estimates. An explanation of the deviations could be included with the report, but these explanations are usually very technical, complex, and often confidential. For these reasons, it is better to explain the differences in a separate letter.

> A research-oriented manufacturer was having difficulty in deciding where to concentrate its research efforts when one or more project objectives were missed. When it adapted the reporting format illustrated in Exhibit 23, the problem was resolved. Effort was concentrated on those projects where the losses were greatest! Within one year this firm was taking share of market from its competitors and increasing its profits to the largest of the firm's history!

Exhibit 24 is an illustration of a summary project report. The summary report lists all active projects which are in process in research and development. The estimated and actual costs for each project are shown, as are the expected completion dates. The cost and physical completion percentages are shown for each project, as well as the project number, project description, and the name of the project manager. Necessary corrective action cannot be determined from this report; however, the report emphasizes those projects where further investigation is required.

The advantages of the summary report are: (1) it is consistent with the pyramidal structure of organizations; (2) it gives a summary report from which additional inquiry can be made; (3) it identifies problem areas as briefly as possible; and (4) it is adaptable to all organizations and can be prepared for any time interval. In this exhibit, for example, the firm's managers would certainly want an explanation for Project 100178 missing its targeted completion date. They would want to know what alternatives are available for correcting the deficiency.

EXHIBIT 23

RESEARCH AND DEVELOPMENT PROJECTS FOR WHICH TARGETS HAVE BEEN MISSED

From 1/1/xx thru 6/1/xx (In Dollars)

Project Number	Project Start Date	Est. Compl. Date	R & D Group	Est. Hours	Est. Cost	% Completion Cost	% Completion Phys.	Actual Cost To Date
100144	2/15/x2	3/15/x2	Design Engr.	150	$ 1,500	100%	100%	$ 1,450
	3/15/x2	4/15/x2	Constr. Engr.	500	25,000	100%	100%	25,000
	4/15/x2	5/15/x2	Exper. Mach. Shop	1000	8,000	90%	90%	7,200
	5/15/x2	7/15/x2	Test Engr.	2000	40,000	10%	10%	4,000
	7/15/x2	8/15/x2	Release	100	1,000	—	—	—
Proj. Total	2/15/x2	8/15/x2		3750	$75,500	49.9%	50%	$ 37,650
100178	4/ 1/x2	4/15/x2	Design Engr.	100	$ 1,000	150%	100%	$ 1,500
	4/15/x2	5/15/x2	Constr. Engr.	1000	50,000	200%	100%	100,000
	5/15/x2	6/15/x2	Exper. Mach. Shop	200	1,600	10%	7.5%	200
	6/15/x2	7/15/x2	Test Engr.	1000	20,000	—	—	—
	7/15/x2	8/ 1/x2	Release	80	800	—	—	—
Proj. Total	4/ 1/x2	8/ 1/x2		2380	$73,400	138.6%	75.6%	$101,700

EXHIBIT 23 (continued)

RESEARCH AND DEVELOPMENT PROJECTS FOR WHICH TARGETS HAVE BEEN MISSED
From 1/1/xx thru 6/1/xx (in Dollars)

Project Number	R & D Group	Projected Total Hours for Compl.	Proj. Cost at Compl.	Proj. Compl. Date	Addl. Hours	Addl. Cost	Gross Margin Lost	Total Cost of Deviation
100144	Design Engr.	145	$ 1,450	4/15/x2	—	—	$2,000	$ 2,000
	Constr. Engr.	500	25,000	6/ 1/x2	—	—	1,000	1,000
	Exper. Mach. Shop	1000	8,000	8/ 1/x2	—	—	2,000	2,000
	Test Engr.	2000	40,000	11/ 1/x2	—	—	2,000	2,000
	Release	100	1,000	12/ 1/x2	—	—	—	—
Proj. Total		3745	$ 75,450	12/ 1/x2	—	—	$7,000	$ 7,000
100178	Design Engr.	150	$ 1,500	5/ 1/x2	50	$ 500	$1,000	$ 1,500
	Constr. Engr.	2000	100,000	6/ 1/x2	1000	50,000	—	50,000
	Exper. Mach. Shop	250	2,000	8/ 1/x2	50	400	2,000	2,400
	Test Engr.	1500	30,000	10/ 1/x2	500	10,000	2,000	12,000
	Release	100	1,000	11/ 1/x2	20	200	1,000	1,200
Proj. Total		4000	$134,500	11/ 1/x2	1620	$61,100	$6,000	$67,100

EXHIBIT 24

SUMMARY RESEARCH AND DEVELOPMENT REPORT
From 1/1/xx thru 6/1/xx

Brief Description	Project Number	Project Start Date	Est. Compl. Date	Est. Hours	Est. Cost	% Completion Cost	% Completion Phys.	Actual Cost To Date
Redesign of Product A	100111	5/ 1/x1	11/15/x1	870	$ 14,500	0.7%	0.7%	$ 100
New product development	100122	3/ 1/x1	11/ 1/x3	5350	114,500	71%	71%	79,500
Cost reduction	100131	2/ 1/x2	7/15/x2	870	16,600	74.7%	75%	12,400
Partial product redesign	100144	2/15/x2	8/15/x2	3750	75,500	49.9%	50%	37,650
New product development	100178	4/ 1/x2	8/ 1/x2	2380	73,400	138.6%	75.6%	101,700

Project Number	Projected Total Hours to Compl.	Project Cost At Completion	Projected Completion Date	Addl. Hours	Addl. Cost	Gross Margin Lost	Total Cost of Deviation
100111	870	$ 14,500	11/15/x2	—	—	—	—
100122	5350	112,000	1/ 1/x3	—	—	—	—
100131	870	16,600	7/15/x2	—	—	—	—
100144	3745	75,450	12/ 1/x2	—	—	$7,000	$ 7,000
100178	4000	134,500	11/ 1/x2	1620	$61,100	6,000	67,100

Chapter 10

Customer Service Ratio Reports

THIS CHAPTER IS AN EXPLANATION OF THE USE OF REPORTING ON CUSTOMER SERVICE RATIOS, including the method of computing the ratios and the advantages of using them. In addition, the effectiveness of customer service ratios as a management control tool is reviewed, such as its flexibility, because reports can be prepared weekly for each product manager for those products for which he is responsible or the weekly reports can be summarized into bi-weekly and/or monthly reports with ratios computed for each level of the organization. Ratios can be reported for managers of product, managers for product families, and by manufacturing location, or summarized for a division of a company!

Customer service ratios are very versatile measures, suitable for all types of business environments. They can be used with and without EDP equipment by large, small or medium-size businesses!

The Mathematics of Customer Service Ratios

Customer service ratios are computed from the number of customers serviced compared to the number of customers who placed orders within a specified period of time. The ratio is usually expressed as a percentage such as a 95 percent customer service ratio.

The ratio is computed by dividing the number of line items shipped for a specified period by the number of line items ordered by customers during the same period. The resulting ratio or percentage is the number of line items shipped as a percentage or ratio of the number ordered. To make this ratio as useful as possible and maintain comparability from period to period, standard assumptions are applied to the computation. For example, if a line on an order is only partially filled, that line item is not considered filled until the total quantity is shipped.

Although such an assumption may not be theoretically correct, it does provide a consistent measure from period to period. It is also less expensive to apply standard assumptions and simplify computing the ratio. A need for comparability requires that the ratio be computed based upon the relationship between the quantities ordered and shipped. By using quantities, price changes are ignored and do not distort the ratios.

Developing Customer Service Ratios in Multi-product Firms with Electronic Data Processing Systems

Manually computing the customer service ratio, for a firm with many products, is impossible. Large orders must be keypunched. The benefits from the use of the customer service ratios easily justify the costs for keypunching. The sales register file or tape is matched against the order input file to identify those items shipped and to compute the ratio.

How to Develop Customer Service Ratios in Multi-product Firms Without Computers

If a computer is not available, or the costs of using one are prohibitive, a sampling technique can be applied. A useful technique is to select two or three products, usually those products with the largest unit sales volume, and at least one product with a medium or low volume. Then sample approximately 10 percent of the orders received against these products each day. Summarize (total) the line items on these orders by two categories, the number filled and unfilled. Divide the total unfilled for the day by the total line items ordered. Subtract the result from 100 percent. The product is the customer service ratio which can be used as a guide for evaluating the effectiveness of the product forecasting and production control responsibilities.

As this ratio is computed and re-computed for each period and compared to the previous ratio, it becomes more valuable as a managing tool. As the sample is consistently applied, the directional trends of the ratio will indicate the source of problems with customer service. The following case illustrates the value of using customer service ratio:

> One leader in its industry computes weekly and monthly customer service ratios which are part of its weekly management reviews. At this meeting actions which have been taken in response to unfavorable trends are discussed. This firm has a low incidence of customer dissatisfaction. A major reason is the consistent use of the customer service ratio. In a period of ten years this firm went from less than 5 percent to over a 45 percent share of the industry market!

Selecting Time Intervals for Computing the Customer Service Ratio

Customer service ratios can be computed for almost any time intervals desired. As a general rule, the faster the feedback, i.e., the shorter the time interval, the faster managers can react and the more effective the use of the ratio.

The ratio can be computed monthly and incorporated in the monthly reporting, or, to be of optimal use, it can be computed daily or weekly. The ratio can be computed for the interval selected and accumulated as weekly, monthly, or year-to-date totals. The period selected is compared to prior periods in the current year and to the same period last year. For example, a weekly ratio is compared to the previous week and the same week last year. The ratio can be accumulated into a monthly total for comparison with last month and the same month of the previous year, plus the accumulated total for the current fiscal year, which can be compared to the same accumulation for the previous fiscal year.

Correlation of the Customer Service Ratio with Customer Problems

The customer service ratio is related to and correlated with the number of customer complaints received about product availability. In addition, there is a correlation between sales returns and allowances and the customer service ratio. The failure to fill orders for one product on time will affect the sales of related products and disrupt a coordinated sales program.

Also, allowances and price concessions may be caused by a failure to meet delivery schedules. Conversely, these concessions will decrease or at least remain at acceptable levels if the customer service ratio required is maintained.

Advantages of Customer Service Ratios As a Management Control Monitor

The Customer Service Ratio Is a Very Flexible Measure

The need for flexibility makes the customer service ratio particularly useful. It can be computed at any desired level. For example, it can be computed for each product, for each product group, for each marketing division, for each sales territory, for each manufacturing location, and each customer or group of customers if desired. The reporting intervals for each of these various groups can be standard or modified for each group. The limitation on the timing, and the groups to which the customer service ratio is applied, are functions of the coding systems available and the availability of data processing equipment. If products, product groups, customers, sales territories, and manufacturing locations are properly coded (such as customer numbers, territory numbers, and manufacturing location numbers), the choice can be made from among almost limitless combinations of alternatives. Without data processing equipment, however, the most that can be expected is two or three small samples of a limited number of categories.

Using Customer Service Ratios To Monitor Customer Service Performance

A consumer goods company computes a customer service ratio for each product for each week. These computations are accumulated for each month and for the fiscal year to date. The current year ratios are compared with last year for the same period. The ratios are computed on data processing equipment. This firm is able to balance its customer service ratios with inventory carrying costs and manufacturing economies and is a leader in its industry in sales and profits! One of the causes of its success is its ability to service its customer promptly!

It Measures Marketing Effectiveness

The customer service ratio is another tool for measuring the effectiveness of the marketing department. For example, a reduction in the ratio, i.e., failure to meet required service levels, indicates the marketing department failed to correctly project the timing and amount of sales of each product. Or, a ratio decrease can indicate a relatively accurate sales forecast, but a failure by marketing to properly balance inventories with shipments and therefore marketing production orders were placed with the manufacturing department too late or the orders were not placed for the correct quantities. Because of the warning from an unfavorable customer service ratio, the reasons for the failure can be investigated.

Improves Service to Customers and Results in More Repeat Sales

A major advantage of the customer service ratio is improved service to customers. The number of stock-outs and partially unfilled items is reduced to an acceptable minimum. More profits accrue to the firm because there are fewer sales lost to competitors due to lack of product availability.

Depending upon the input used to compute the customer service ratio, a list of customers and products, for example, which are back-ordered can be prepared in the computer at the time the line items ordered are matched against inventory for order filling. A crosscheck of this list with previous lists can indicate areas where there are continous problems. The crosschecking can also be programmed and done on a computer. Once problem products, manufacturing locations, or customers are identified, an investigation can be made to find the cause and corrective action initiated. This action, if taken immediately, can prevent loss of customers and loss of market share for the product or products affected.

The customer service ratio is a necessary ingredient for establishing required inventory levels. The inventory levels are a balance between the desired customer service ratios, the costs of carrying the inventory, the manufacturing lead time required to manufacture the product, and the economic production quantity for that product. The cost factors for determining product levels are insufficient for establishing inventory without the input from marketing in the form of the customer service level desired.

Pinpoints Chronic Problems

The customer service ratio is particularly useful for identifying recurring problems. For example, are the declining ratios concentrated in a particular sales territory? If so, the effect upon market share in that territory could be disastrous. The causes could be poor forecasting in that territory or failure to forward and process orders from that territory on a timely basis.

A poor ratio may be concentrated in a particular product, or product group. A concentration in a product or product group can materially affect market share. The problem can be caused by failure to accurately forecast sales for those products or because the forecast is not synchronized with the demand for the product.

The failure, if related to a group of products, could be caused by poor forecasts from a marketing group or section. If this problem persists, it will be necessary to change personnel within the marketing group which is responsible for the forecast.

An unacceptable customer service ratio could be caused by a failure within manufacturing. If the products with the poor service ratios are produced in one or two manufacturing facilities, the problems could be in the manufacturing process, i.e., a failure to produce sufficient acceptable products or the lack of available manufacturing capacity for that product. Because of the internal reward structure, manufacturing could consistently refuse to devote enough capacity to the product, if, for example, manufacturing is unable to manufacture the product at the assigned standard cost.

If a product or product group has a consistently low customer service ratio, the pricing must be reviewed. The products may be priced too low relative to competitors, or they may be priced below what the "market will bear." In that case, it is doubtful that supply would never reach demand!

Remedial Action

A manufacturer discovered a low customer service ratio persisted within a group of products. A review of the pricing indicated a 5 percent relative price incrcase could be made. The customer service ratio increased to acceptable levels and the manufacturer captured a larger share of market as well as a share of its competitor's profits!

Determining Managerial Corrective Action to Unfavorable Customer Service Ratio Reports to Reduce Lost Sales

Depending on the information available, a broad range of corrective reactions is possible. One such reaction could include a shift of advertising effort from products with low ratios to products with higher ratios. The faster the unfavorable trends are recognized, the more likely the advertising program can be revised. If the trends are recognized too late, the advertising funds will have been committed and the result is an emphasis upon the wrong products.

If the advertising effort is successfully shifted, it will decrease the demand for the product with the low customer service ratio; thereby reducing the line items ordered without affecting availability, and thereby increasing the value of the customer service ratio. On the other hand, the shift will increase the demand, i.e., line items ordered, for products with high ratios, causing an increase in unfilled items and a decrease in the customer service ratio. The net result is fewer lost sales!

Another Cure for an Unacceptable Ratio

A more difficult to implement, but effective, reaction to unacceptable customer service ratios is a change in the manufacturing or production schedule. This would increase product availability but cause a delay in delivery dates, which would result in the loss of some customers, but not as many as would be lost if no action were taken.

In any event, a review of the pricing policy is necessary. A sure way to reduce the demand and thereby the "stock-outs" is to increase the product price. It is necessary to test the market to find the "right" price and usually even a small price increase will cause a loss of customers as well as volume. In addition, or as an alternative, the price of a substitute product can be decreased, shifting demand to that product.

If there are a number of substitute products, the prices of more than one should be decreased to dissipate the demand and not transfer the problem of "stock-outs" from one product to another. It is often possible to meet the product demand with more than one substitute, and a slight price decrease will usually make the substitutes acceptable.

Analysis of Corrective Action

Before any corrective action is taken, an analysis of the various alternatives is made to determine the most profitable. The costs and benefits of each alternative are summarized and compared to identify the alternative with the most benefits and the least cost.

For example, the gross margin forgone on the lost sales is compared to: (a) the expected gross margin from a price increase; or (b) the gross margin expected to be lost by decreasing the prices of substitutes (to determine the least loss); or (c) the incremental costs of disrupting the manufacturing schedule to make more products available; or (d) the carrying costs of increasing the size of the inventory.

If it is more profitable to forgo the gross margin on lost sales, then that is the alternative which is selected.

Results to be Gained from Using Customer Service Ratio Reports on a Regular Basis

Reporting on the customer service ratio builds profits because a change in ratio causes managers to act before excessive losses occur. The immediate recognition of a trend results in action *before* the problem becomes serious and many customers are lost to competitors. The reaction of the firm is planned, which means managers can influence the result, rather than be subject to the whims of chance! The problem is severe only if *no* action is taken.

In short, the reported customer service ratio becomes a standard against which to measure performance, and a measure of the current status of customer service, as well as an indicator of a problem, before that problem becomes too serious. The customer service ratio is a protector of customers and profits!

Illustrations of the Computation and Reporting of Customer Service Ratios

The first illustration is taken from a manufacturer with a large product line who sells large volumes of each product. In order to get the most benefit from the ratios, they are reported weekly and computed on automatic data processing equipment. When the report was published, the ratios which indicated unfavorable trends were subject to detailed analysis. (Exhibit 25)

The customer service ratio is accumulated each week for each fiscal year. The ratio is included in the weekly review of key business indicators.

Illustration Number 2 (Exhibit 26) is taken from a seasonal business and the ratio is computed monthly only during the selling season. The ratio is computed on data processing equipment and reviewed monthly for the five months of each selling season by the financial managers. Any unfavorable trends are analyzed and reported to the responsible executives for corrective action.

ILLUSTRATION #1 (EXHIBIT 25)

CUSTOMER SERVICE RATIOS
For the Week Ended 6/12/xx

Description	Budget[2] or Objective	For the[3] Week 6/12/xx	For the Previous Week	For the Same Week LY	For the Month of June xx	For the Month of May xx	For June of LY thru Same Week
Product A	95.0	96.3	96.1	94.0	96.0	94.4	94.0
Product AA	86.0	85.4	84.8	86.1	85.0	86.1	86.0
Product B	70.0	68.1	66.0	64.1	68.2	65.4	64.2
Product C	90.0	88.6	87.7	88.4	89.1	88.3	88.8
Product D	80.0	81.1	80.9	79.9	81.2	78.8	79.6
Product E	80.0	80.7	80.1	78.9	80.8	78.7	78.0
Product FF	80.0	77.9	76.6	72.2	77.8	75.6	71.1
Product G	75.0	74.0	73.4	74.0	74.1	74.0	73.0
Product H	85.0	84.0	84.0	85.0	83.3	84.6	86.0
Product I	90.0	91.1	90.0	90.0	89.9	90.0	91.3
Product M	95.0	95.0	94.4	94.0	94.0	94.7	94.1
Product N	98.0	95.0	96.7	97.8	95.9	97.7	96.7
Product O	80.0	80.9	82.1	81.2	81.1	81.4	89.1
Product Group L	84.0	83.6	80.7	83.8	84.3	83.9	82.9
Lincoln Mfg. Location	80.0	76.6	75.3	78.9	76.8	79.7	79.8

(1)The ratio is initially computed weekly, which is the same as the billing cycle.

(2)The budget is based upon last year modified by expected changes.

(3)The computation can include an order and item more than once, because if unfilled it is re-submitted, and appears in a later ratio and twice in the cumulative ratio. However, if processed consistently from period to period, the trend will be valid, provided there is not a substantial change in the method and priorities assigned for processing back orders.

EXHIBIT 25 (continued)

CUSTOMER SERVICE RATIOS
For the Week Ended 6/12/xx

Description	Cumulative TY thru W/E 6/12/xx	Cumulative LY thru Same Week	Comments[1]
Product A	97.0	95.1	Orders were less than expected.
Product AA	83.1	85.8	Meeting objectives.
Product B	63.3	61.0	Orders are exceeding expectations.
Product C	88.4	88.8	Not materially different from plan.
Product D	81.1	79.9	Product price will be checked.
Product E	80.0	80.0	Advertising emphasis will be re-examined.
Product FF	74.9	77.5	Forecast will be adjusted.
Product G	71.6	74.6	Substantially on target.
Product H	83.2	84.8	Not significantly deviating from plan.
Product I	91.1	88.8	This product will be watched for a trend.
Product M	94.6	95.0	Meeting objectives.
Product N	96.3	98.0	The objective should be re-examined; ratio is too high.
Product O	80.0	80.1	Meeting objectives.
Product Group L	82.4	86.2	Although close to the objectives, the ratio is substantially below last year and the causes must be identified.
Lincoln Mfg. Location	74.8	70.1	On a cumulative basis, this location is not meeting the objectives. A project team must be sent to investigate the reasons.

[1] Where necessary, the comments are usually followed up with a report because the problems must be thoroughly investigated and resolved or the customer service ratio will deteriorate further.

ILLUSTRATION #2 (EXHIBIT 26)

CUSTOMER SERVICE RATIOS
Through the Week Ended 6/12/xx

Description	Budget[2] or Objective	For the[3] Week 6/12/xx	For the Previous Week	For the[4] Same Week L/S	For the Month of June xx	For the Month of May xx	For the Same Week & Month L/S
Material 100165	95.0	95.2	95.1	90.0	95.1	95.2	91.0
Material 100318	90.0	60.0	58.7	90.0	60.2	59.7	90.7
Material 100219	95.0	80.0	80.0	77.0	79.6	80.0	76.8
Material 100172	95.0	94.6	95.7	61.0	96.1	95.0	60.0
Material 100177	90.0	81.0	80.0	96.3	82.1	80.8	96.1
Material 100144	85.0	85.6	85.0	84.4	86.0	85.4	84.0
Material 100145	80.0	95.0	95.0	90.0	93.9	94.1	91.2
Material 100146	90.0	50.0	51.0	95.2	49.6	50.0	95.5
Material 100147	90.0	90.0	90.0	90.0	90.0	90.0	90.0
Material 100149	95.0	94.7	95.0	94.4	94.0	95.1	94.0
Material 100511	95.0	98.3	98.2	99.9	98.2	98.2	99.6
Material 100521	95.0	96.1	96.0	90.5	96.0	96.0	90.0

(1) The ratio is computed weekly during the season at the time orders from customers are processed for release to manufacturing.

(2) The budget or objective is based, each season, upon the judgment of the marketing executives about what can be accomplished with each material. Objectives are set only on materials which are expected to sell in significant quantities, and only those materials are reported on.

(3) Under these conditions, an order and line item appear only in each material's computation once. Although it is possible to re-order, that is an unusual case. Usually the material is not available to complete the order and a substitute would not be recommended unless it were available. If no acceptable substitute is available, because of the seasonality, the order is canceled.

(4) The materials purchased from season to season are rarely identical. Therefore, materials of similar design, color and construction are chosen as comparators from the previous season. The selection is judgmental in nature and must be used judiciously.

EXHIBIT 26 (continued)

CUSTOMER SERVICE RATIOS
Through the Week Ended 6/12/xx

Description	Cumulative T/S thru W/E 6/12/xx	Cumulative L/S thru Same Week	Comments[1]
Material 100165	95.0	90.7	This material is meeting objectives because it is not selling.
Material 100318	60.1	90.7	This material is outselling expectations; most orders will not be filled.
Material 100219	80.0	76.1	The demand for this material was underestimated.
Material 100172	96.7	58.2	The sales of this material are meeting expectations and objectives.
Material 100177	79.4	96.0	This material could not be purchased in the quantities forecast.
Material 100144	85.6	84.4	This material is meeting objective.
Material 100145	94.1	90.9	This material has a high ratio because it is not selling.
Material 100146	49.0	95.5	The demand for this material was underestimated by at least 50%.
Material 100147	90.0	90.0	The sales of this material are meeting expectations.
Material 100149	94.6	94.4	This material is meeting objective.
Material 100511	98.1	99.1	This material is not selling, therefore there is adequate availability. It should be considered for markdown.
Material 100521	95.5	90.0	The sales, and therefore availability, of this product are on target.

[1] The financial executives review this report, investigate causes, and then issue a report to top management. The report contains recommended action and is issued rapidly because of the shortness of the season. The purpose of the report is to prevent loss of customers and sales which will result in decreased profits! In these circumstances, a low customer service ratio can indicate a material has "caught on" and is selling much more than expected. Because it is a seasonal business, the possibility of re-ordering is rare. On the other hand, a high ratio may mean the material is a "flop" and all orders received can be easily filled. The seasonability of the market requires quick reaction to protect sales and profits and prevent a "bottom line" disaster!

Chapter 11

How to Use Distribution Sampling Reports for Improved Planning And More Profits

What Is Distribution Sampling?

Distribution sampling is the periodic physical counting of a manufacturer's products in his customers' warehouses. The purpose is the identification of the inventory and sales of the manufacturer's products one step earlier in the distribution process. Through the sample, the manufacturer can: (a) control his inventory investment, (b) smooth his manufacturing schedule, and (c) increase profits and return on investment in inventory.

25% Edge in Return on Inventory Investment

A leader in its industry regularly samples the inventories of its customers. Because of this technique, the firm earns a higher return on its inventory than its competitors! This firm closely matches inventory investment and sales; minimizes manufacturing setup costs and almost eliminates the costs of employee turnover! The return on inventory investment is 25 percent greater than its nearest competitor!

What to Include in the Sample

The sample must include the manufacturer's key customers and products in each sales territory. The characteristics of the territory must be included in the sample. The customers included in the sample must represent all customers in that sales territory and the products must represent the largest sellers in the territory. The measure needed from the sample is the inventory turn by customer, product, and territory.

Arriving at Customer's Sales

The sales needed for calculating the inventory turn is a rolling twelve-month total of the customer's sales for the products sampled. The rolling sales estimate is the total of the customer's latest month's sales and twelve-months cumulative sales from which is subtracted the earliest month's sales to arrive at an updated twelve-months rolling sales estimate. If twelve-months sales history is not available for that customer, then the available sales are summed and multiplied by an annualizing factor. A factor is also used to calculate total customer sales from the sample. The total annualized sales, divided by the inventory equals the inventory turn.

The product inventory value is computed the same as sales. It is computed by adjusting the sample inventory by a factor to equal the customer's (distributor's) total inventory.

If the distributor represents the territory, an inventory turn for the territory is easily calculated by dividing the distributor's inventory by the estimated percentage his inventories are to the total inventories for the territory. The result is a total territory inventory. By applying the same method to the distributor's sales, a total territory sales is calculated. Dividing the total sales by the inventory is the estimated territory turn.

Use of Inventory Turn

After the inventory turn is computed, it should be compared with at least the last six turns to identify trends. Once a trend has been identified (it is possible no trend will be indicated), then a plan of action can be initiated.

Assume a downward trend in the turn is identified, i.e., the inventory turn is decreasing. The inventory levels at the manufacturer's regional warehouses must be adjusted to reduce the inventory of products affected. The trend may cause a complete adjustment of inventories or it may be limited to a regional adjustment. If a total adjustment is needed, the manufacturing schedule should be reviewed in detail. The manufacturing schedule must be changed by either lowering the quantities to be manufactured or by completely eliminating the products affected from the current schedule.

If the decreasing turn affects only a region or a territory, products inventories can be shifted between territories. The transfer of inventories will balance regional inventory turns and thus increase customer service and profits.

In addition, any action plan must go further, to the raw materials used to manufacture those products. The quantities of raw materials inventories are reduced by either canceling orders or diverting the raw materials to other products by adjusting the manufacturing schedule. The result of a quick reaction is a reduced investment in raw materials and an increased return on the assets used in the business!

Benefits from Distribution Sampling

The most important benefits are: (a) lower interest costs because of a reduction in the investment in inventories; (b) lower manufacturing costs because of better planning; and (c) lower cyclical swings causing less employee turnover. The result is maximization of return on capital employed in the business and of return from the investment in inventory. By timing the sampling to support the next planning cycle, plans can be based upon data from one step ahead in the distribution cycle. For example, the sales forecast is no longer dependent upon the history of the manufacturer's sales and orders received. The forecast can be modified by conditions which exist at the next and earlier level of distribution.

The effect upon the sales forecast is to make it less volatile and more reliable. Changes in the demand for the manufacturer's products are detected earlier and the manufacturing schedule can be adjusted quickly. The early information will smooth the manufacturing schedule, eliminating the need for reducing then increasing personnel to meet production requirements.

Manufacturing will have time to make adjustments with minimum cost. The ability to adjust the sales forecast and manufacturing schedule quickly will smooth out inventory balances and increase profits by at least the prime rate multiplied by the decrease in inventory balances!

Continued Profits Possible in Volatile Markets

During the 1974 recession a sudden drop in small tool orders caused losses and resulted in excess inventories for all firms in an industry but one. That firm not only avoided a loss, but continued to increase its profits 10 percent with no excess inventories! The reason: It was sampling the market a step ahead in the distribution cycle and a step ahead of its competition!

Continuously adjusting the manufacturing schedule within short intervals is costly. Early knowledge eliminates the unexpected shifting of the manufacturing facilities from one product to another. The reduction of turbulence in the manufacturing cycle decreases setup costs by eliminating switching from product to product for short production runs.

Overtime is reduced because the shifting of the manufacturing resources is planned rather than reactive. Both "stock outs" and surpluses of critical raw materials, and excess or shortages of personnel are eliminated. In short, the benefits of distribution sampling are reduced manufacturing and inventory costs with increased profits.

How to Build and Use Samples of Distributors' Inventories

The first step is the division of the national sales area into territories. The technique most often used is to divide the national area into almost equal geographic territories. However, territories of equal geographic size may not be comparable economically. Therefore, territories may be established which are approximately equal in volume for the largest selling products. This method can create large geographic territories because of the differences between geography and the population distribution. But for purposes of profit measurement it is more important to emphasize economic contribution than geographic distribution.

Selecting the Sample

Dividing the total sales area into relatively equal economic territories establishes comparability and norms against which to measure progress. Within each territory select customers (distributors) who are the most representative. These are usually the largest customers within a territory.

In some territories, the choice is easy—there is only one large jobber. In other territories, however, there may be two or more customers of almost equal size. In that situation, choose jobbers (distributors) whose sales include the widest product distribution, that is, those jobbers whose sales are not concentrated in one product or group of products.

If, in some territories, there are many distributors of approximately equal size, select two or three distributors whose sales approximate the product distribution for the whole territory. This procedure will result in the selection of a representative sample.

Incentives for Customer Participation

Usually, distributors (customers) will not participate in such a program voluntarily. It is necessary to offer an incentive for them to participate. The incentive may be extra product at a bargain price or a special gift. It could also be a combination of specially priced merchandise and gifts. Without incentives, do not expect customers to be interested. However, once the participating distributors are identified, then the products must be selected.

Selection of the Products to be Sampled

The product sample selected must represent the largest selling products in the sales territory. As a general rule, 10 to 15 percent of the participating customers' inventory, including the largest selling products in that territory, should be part of the sample. To select the products, the estimated inventory for each customer chosen is reviewed in detail until the sample percentage is reached.

> After using this procedure for one year, Leslie Plastics discovered that it had a smoothing effect upon inventory balances, sales projections, and manufacturing costs. The result of distribution sampling for this firm was a higher return on inventory investment, more accurate sales projections and lower manufacturing costs! These results increased profit by more than 5 percent per annum!

Estimating Distributors' (Customers') Sales

The next step in the sampling process is estimating distributors' sales for one year to the inventory date. Distributors' sales are estimated by adding the net shipments to the customer for the current month to the customers' inventory at the end of the previous month. From this total deduct the customers' current product inventory. The result is what the customer (distributor) has sold that month. (The distributors' monthly inventories are calculated from the periodic sampling.) The calculated sales for the current month are added to the cumulative total. Then, the sales for the oldest month are dropped off; the result is a rolling twelve-month forecast for each distributor.

If this is the first forecast for this distributor, a yearly forecast is calculated by annualizing the current month's sales, i.e., multiplying the current month's sales by 12 or by a factor which after adjustment for seasonal variations is equal to twelve months' sales. After actual sales experience is accumulated for each distributor the monthly sales are substituted for the calculated sales.

Computing the Inventory Turn

Both the product sales and inventory have been estimated; now the inventory turn can be computed. The inventory is divided into the calculated sales for each customer and product to compute the inventory turn. The calculated turn is the substitute for the actual inventory turn for that product, territory, and customer. If the manufacturer's sales records are up to date, differences between the actual and calculated inventory turn will not be significant.

Analysis of the Inventory Turn

One sample inventory turn is not very useful. The turn is of most benefit if it is part of a trend. If possible, at least six months of turns should be compared. In addition, to the inventory turn, the sales trend is analyzed to identify the slope of the sales curve. The analyses are an attempt to discover: (a) whether the product, distributor, and territory sales are increasing, decreasing, or remaining stable? (b) whether the inventories are increasing, decreasing, or remaining relatively stable? and (c) how do the inventory levels and mix compare with accumulated history? Any changes identified will affect the manufacturer's projections, therefore, the comparison and evaluation must be detailed and accurate.

If the sample inventory turn is increasing, i.e., the inventory is moving faster than recent trends, it is necessary to increase the resources devoted to manufacturing those products affected (assuming the manufacturer's inventory of those products is not in an overstock position). Avoiding "stock outs" by increasing production will increase profits and more than offset the costs of sampling. If, on the other hand, the inventory turn is decreasing, production schedules must be adjusted downward to avoid excess inventory which causes increased storage costs, handling, investment, and distress pricing. Because sampling provides information upon which to act quickly and prevent these costs, profits increase!

Inventory Sampling Replaces Customer Orders as a Basis for Planning

The information derived from sampling is more useful for planning than customer orders. Sampling relates customer sales to customer inventories. Customer orders are received too late and are dependent upon factors which do not necessarily relate to supply and demand.

For example, orders may reflect the short-run cash position of the distributor or his short-run sales and cash forecasts. Distributors may be withholding orders because of expectations of more favorable terms of purchase in the near future. Also, the customer may withhold orders because he is resisting current prices and point of sale incentives. The timing of a customer's order may depend more upon the influence of the manufacturer's salesman than need for the product or it may depend upon the degree of sophistication of the customer.

Some distributors will not recognize their need for a product until they reach the point of "stock out." Others have effective inventory systems and order as needed. Because, in many cases, orders from customers are more dependent upon their absolute rather than relative inventory position and the type of product they sell, the inventory sample is more accurate and useful to the manufacturer as a planning tool than are actual orders! The manufacturer can be, and must be, ahead of his competition!

Projections from the Sample

From the sample, the manufacturer can project sales by customer and product for each territory. The projection is necessarily naive because it is based upon a recent history of inventory turns. The information for plotting the trend line is directly available from the samples. One axis on the graph is time and the other is sales.

For example, the territory projection is calculated from the projection by distributor (customer). If the sample consists of one customer whose sales are 10 percent of the territory sales, the customer's projected sales are divided by 10 percent to arrive at the projected sales for that territory. If the sample includes more than one customer, the projections are totaled and divided by the sum of the percentages of the customer sales to the total sales for that territory.

The projections by product are summarized in the same manner as those by customer. The product sales are projected using a trend line. The projections for each product are summed and divided by the percentage these products are of the total territory sales. The territory sales projected by product should not materially differ from the territory sales calculated from the customer projections.

Preparing the Manufacturing Schedule

Once the total sales by product are projected, the manufacturer's current product inventory levels are deducted to compute the quantities to be manufactured. From this calculation a tentative manufacturing schedule is prepared. The manufacturing schedule is prepared for the next six-months selling season with enough flexibility in scheduling to revise the plan if changes are indicated by future samples.

After the manufacturing schedule is established, it must be disaggregated into a bill of materials and product build schedules from which the labor hours, raw materials, purchased parts and manufacturing supplies needed to meet the schedule are estimated. The quantities of these resources needed to meet the manufacturing schedule are adjusted for raw material, parts, and supply inventories. The remainder is the purchasing plan which is tentative and subject to adjustment.

> The reduction in raw material and supply inventories is important to profit in a manufacturing environment! In one case, any increase in scrap above the 1 percent parts scrap allowance means a decrease in profits equal to 5 times the excess of the actual scrap over that allowed! However, a simple analysis indicated that a smoothing of the raw materials and parts inventories caused a saving that exceeded any historical losses from excess scrap! Sampling was initiated, the savings were realized and profits increased 17 percent over the previous period!

Illustration of the Use of a Sample

The manufacturer divided its selling area, the continental United States, into 20 sales territories. Within each territory, distributors were listed by estimated sales of the manufacturer's products. Distributors were selected by sales volume; those with the largest sales volume were listed first, then those with the next largest volume until the combined sales equaled 10 percent of the sales of the manufacturer's products in the territory. During the selection process it was attempted not to choose distributors who were geographically contiguous, that is, separated from one another only by an imaginary territory boundary.

From each distributor, 20 percent of the manufacturer's products sold by them were selected and included in the sample. After selecting the sample, the manufacturer organized inventory teams and sent them to meet his salesman. Each team included one member from central marketing, one from finance, and the salesman assigned to that customer.

This manufacturer has, in the past, taken the sample monthly. If, however, the total selling area cannot be covered by no more than two inventory teams within a month, the inventory schedule must be revised to sample each territory on a cyclical basis, such as every two or three months. For example, the sample can be scheduled to complete all territories once every three months. Using this procedure, the sales and inventory turn data for each territory would be updated every quarter instead of monthly. This should still result in timely, useful information. Examples of the reports which can be used are illustrated at the end of this chapter (Exhibits 27 and 28).

How to Calculate the Sample, Sales, and Inventory

To calculate the total territory sales from the sample, the sample sales are divided by the percentage the sample sales are of the territory total sales; for example, if the sample sales by a distributor are 10 percent of the territory total and equal $100,000, the estimated total territory sales will equal $1,000,000. If the product sample equaled $100,000 and is 10 percent of the total territory product sales the total territory sales equal $1,000,000. This amount is the same as that estimated from the distributor sample. The same procedure is followed to compute the total inventories from the sample. If the sample is 10 percent of the distributor's inventory, the total sample is assumed to be 10 percent of the territory inventory after factoring for the relative size of distributors.

EXAMPLE #1 (EXHIBIT 27) AN EXAMPLE OF A REPORT ON A DISTRIBUTION SAMPLE

For The Month Of July 19XX

	Inventory Turn						
Description	Feb.	March	April	May	June	Current Month	Comments
Territory #5:							
Distributor A:							
Product #1	9.1	9.2	9.0	9.0	9.1	9.1	Change Not Significant
Product #2	12.5	12.6	12.3	12.5	12.7	12.6	Change Not Significant
Product #3	10.4	10.4	10.3	10.4	10.8	10.9	Checking this territory for product availability.
Territory #6:							
Distributor A:							
Product #1	9.2	9.2	9.1	9.1	9.2	9.2	Change Not Significant
Product #3	10.0	10.1	10.0	10.1	10.0	10.0	Change Not Significant
Distributor B:							
Product #1	8.1	8.0	8.0	8.0	8.0	8.1	Change Not Significant
Product #2	12.1	12.1	12.1	11.9	12.2	12.0	Change Not Significant
Product #3	9.9	9.9	10.0	9.9	9.2	8.1	This decrease is being investigated and the amount of this product in this territory is being checked to avoid inventory losses.

EXAMPLE #1—EXHIBIT 27—(Continued)

AN EXAMPLE OF A REPORT ON A DISTRIBUTION SAMPLE
For The Month Of July 19XX

	Inventory Turn						
Description	Feb.	March	April	May	June	Current Month	Comments
Territory #8:							
Distributor A:							
Product #1	8.9	8.9	8.8	8.8	8.8	8.9	Change Not Significant
Product #2	12.1	12.2	12.3	12.2	12.0	12.1	Change Not Significant
Distributor B:							
Product #6	11.1	11.0	11.0	11.0	10.1	8.9	See Product Summary
Product Summary:							
Product #1	9.0	9.1	9.0	9.1	9.1	9.0	Change Not Significant
Product #2	12.1	12.0	12.1	12.1	12.0	12.1	Change Not Significant
Product #3	10.1	10.1	10.1	10.0	10.1	10.1	Change Not Significant
Product #6	11.4	11.3	11.2	11.1	10.0	8.8	This decrease is being investigated and all inventories and manufacturing schedules reviewed to avoid over stocking in this product.

The inventory turn is simply the product of the sales divided by the inventory amount. The inventory turn is a flexible criterion. The turn can be computed by customer, by territory or product, and by product group. The change in inventory turn is the statistic needed for forecasting. If the inventory turn is decreasing, the sales forecast should be reduced by a similar percentage. In addition, reductions should be made in projected finished goods inventories, in the manufacturing schedule, and in orders for purchased parts and raw materials.

Summary

The need for a manufacturer to anticipate changes in the sales of his products is necessary for maximum profit. Early recognition of a change in sales avoids "stock outs" and excess inventories. Through sampling inventories a step ahead in the distribution cycle, the manufacturer is aware of changes in the demand for his products before the changes are reflected in orders received.

Because of this knowledge, the manufacturer can adjust his sales forecast and manufacturing resources to the new sales level. And he can make these adjustments before his competitors. The result of this quick adjuustment is increased profits while competitors are facing losses. The increase in profits is equal to the savings in inventory investment plus the savings in manufacturing cost and the costs of personnel turnover.

EXAMPLE #2 (EXHIBIT 28)

APPLICATION OF THE INFORMATION REPORTED IN EXAMPLE #1

This report was prepared because of the decrease in inventory turn for Product #6 reported in Example #1. The investigation indicated that the decrease in inventory turn for Product #6 was caused by both an increase in customers' inventories and a decrease in customers' sales. The following information was summarized for management from current and prior reports: (a) inventories of Product #6 from the sample of July 19XX $100,000; (b) customer sales from the same sample $880,000; (c) dividing (a) into (b) results in the current inventory turn of 8.8 times; and (d) historical information which indicates a trend of:

DISTRIBUTION SAMPLE
PRODUCT #6 19XX

Description	April	May	June
Sales	$1,019,000	$1,000,000	$900,000
Inventory	$ 90,000	$ 90,000	$ 90,000
Turn	11.2	11.1	10.0

Because of this trend an inquiry was made to determine the amount of inventories of Product #6 at the manufacturer's regional warehouses. From the answers received the managers concluded that the quantities of Product #6 in the regional warehouses were not excessive.

After reviewing all the data the manufacturer's managers had to decide whether the deterioration in inventory turn was a short or long-range phenomenon. They decided it was long-range. Because their customers' sales of Product #6 had decreased by 12.9 percent from April to July, management ordered a 13.0 percent decrease in the manufacturing schedule for the remainder of the fiscal year.

The report illustrated in Example 1 resulted in the investigation, report, and reaction described here. The manufacturer's managers, applying judgment to the facts revealed in the reports, reacted before any change occurred in orders received from their customers. This quick reaction reduced manufacturing costs and preserved the manufacturer's "Bottom Line."

Chapter 12

Use Your Reports for Total Cost Control

The Reports Recommended in This Book Cover All Costs

If all of the reports described in this book are used, the managers will have a complete picture of the cost effectiveness of their firm. The reports cover all manufacturing costs, the costs of marketing the product, research and development costs, and all discretionary costs, including the costs of executives, accountants, personnel specialists, and all other support groups. Some of the reports are specialized such as the frozen standard cost report which emphasizes manufacturing costs, but use of all the reports will cover all costs. If all of these reports are consistently applied, the firm will increase its profit!

Reports for Controlling Manufacturing Costs

A small reduction in the cost of a high-volume product can substantially increase profits. Therefore, in manufacturing, the identification and reporting of small changes in unit costs is imperative. In addition, managers must decide what the unit manufacturing cost of a product should be. The best guide for identifying the ideal product cost is the frozen standard.

Frozen Standard Reporting Is an Exacting Guide to Continuous Product Cost Control

Frozen standard cost reporting emphasizes the variation in product costs from the most desirable levels. Because the report includes the current unit standard cost, the actual unit cost, and the original (frozen) standard unit cost (which was developed when the product was introduced), the firm's managers have a complete picture of the product's cost status.

The effect of inefficiency and inflation on product unit manufacturing costs can easily be measured from the report. The frozen standard tells management what has happened since the product was developed. The effects of inaction upon unit manufacturing costs are disclosed.

Managers need only glance at the report and they can identify areas of neglect. They know where cost control has been lacking. Through the report the most effective control information possible for product unit cost is available.

Control of Marketing's Contribution Requires a Flexible Approach

The contribution of marketing to a firm's sucess can be measured and controlled in at least two ways. First, the volume of sales produced by marketing can be increased while holding operating costs relatively stable or the sales volume can be held constant while operating costs are reduced.

Three Steps for Reporting on Marketing Programs to Increase Their Success

The first and most important reporting step for controlling marketing's contribution is to include in the reporting system the objective sought from the marketing program. If the objective is met or exceeded, then control has been achieved. The report on the progress of the marketing program keeps the objective in front of management at all times.

The second necessary reporting step is to report the actual results achieved and compare it to the plan. The inclusion of both the results achieved and the plan makes it easy for management to follow the progress that has been made. However, to make the report truly effective, the variances from the plan are included in the report. This further simplifies the report for management. Deviations from objectives are highlighted.

The third important step is to include the results of the investigation of the variances in the report. For managers to react to the report, they must know what caused the deviations. The reasons for the variations are indentified in the investigative stage and are the fuel for the managers' decisions. These three steps comprise a complete report which can assure the firm of the contribution needed from marketing to maintain and increase profits.

The Use of Customer Service Ratios to Decrease Lost Sales

The report on customer service ratios is an easy tool for managers to use to evaluate the changes in, and the level of, service to customers. A customer that does not receive service is usually a customer that will be lost. Profits cannot be recognized until a sale is made. If the customer and sale are lost, so is the profit.

However, good customer service can increase sales and therefore profits. Reporting on customer service is a technique managers can use to control the level of sales volume. If the level of sales sought is achieved, the expected contribution from marketing will be achieved.

If, however, the customer service ratio needed is not achieved, sales will decrease and operating costs must be decreased to maintain profits. The change in the customer service ratio is a leading indicator telling managers that action to reduce operating costs is necessary. The quicker operating costs are reduced, the less they must be reduced.

The Effect of Discretionary Costs upon Profits

With the increase in automation of the factory, discretionary costs become more important. Discretionary costs include such costs as general management, accounting, personnel, purchasing, information systems, experimental engineering, and quality control. These costs are classified as general and administrative costs. Discretionary costs also include manufacturing engineering, material handling, manufacturing supplies, plant maintenance and repair, and energy and power. These costs are classified as factory administrative costs. Furthermore, discretionary costs include the costs of sales managers, advertising, product managers, and sales program planners. These costs are classified as marketing and selling costs. The total of these types of costs can range from 20 percent to 80 percent of a firm's total costs. Because of their magnitude, these costs can cause losses or significantly reduce profits.

Discretionary costs are particularly hard to control. These costs cannot be directly related to any measures of productivity. Therefore, the level of these costs required is almost indeterminate. Managers are constantly searching for ways to determine whether or not the level of these costs is adequate or excessive.

Three Cost Control Benefits of Break-even Analysis Reporting

Because break-even analysis reporting includes the percentage of contribution margin, it is simple to compute the sales needed to cover any increase in discretionary costs. By making this simple computation, managers can decide whether sales can be increased sufficiently to cover any increase in discretionary costs and maintain the level of profits.

The second cost control benefit of break-even analysis is that it not only indicates the point of no profits, but the effect upon that point of varying levels of discretionary costs. Managers are aware of the margin of safety and the degree of risk they can take. The report is a visual display of the impact of discretionary costs. The result of reviewing the report is usually a decision to reduce costs and change the break-even point.

In addition, if the break-even report is used as recommended, it will indicate the break-even trend of the firm. The simple break-even point becomes obsolete so quickly that the trend is more relevant for decisions. If the trend is unfavorable, then action is necessary to reduce discretionary costs before losses are incurred. If the break-even trend is favorable, current policies can be continued. Regardless of the directional trend, managers will know what it is and use it as input for their decisions.

The Use of Incremental Cost Analysis Reporting for Better Cost Control

Incremental cost analysis emphasizes the effect of cost variability upon decisions. This report accents the costs that increase and decrease with each management decision. The report also indicates those costs that are unaffected by a decision.

The report tells management to what extent incremental contributions will increase profits if discretionary costs are held constant. If discretionary costs are cut, the incremental contribution plus the decrease in discretionary costs will fall through to the "bottom line." If the discretionary costs are held constant while volume is increased, the firm will be trading on or leveraging its internal fixed costs and increasing its profits. Again, this report emphasizes the benefits from controlling discretionary costs. Often, the effect of incremental costs upon profits is known, but the effect of discretionary costs is overlooked. If an incremental analysis indicates a net contribution, by sharply curtailing discretionary spending, the net contribution will directly increase profits!

Zero Based Budgeting—an Important Cost Control Tool

Because of the difficulty with measuring and controlling discretionary costs, zero based budgeting developed as a control method. Zero based budgeting puts the managers of discretionary cost departments in the position of competing with outside services. Therefore, they become more efficient. If these departments cannot perform their services for at least the same cost as those outside the firm, they will perish. The users of these services will purchase them outside the firm and the internal services will eventually be eliminated. Zero based budgeting is particularly suited for discretionary cost departments such as maintenance and data processing.

An additional benefit is that the managers of departments such as maintenance and data processing will learn about cost control and the need for, and effect of, productivity. These managers are usually surprised by the degree of improvement they can make in their operations once they are given responsibility for total results. Zero based budgeting, by eliminating captive markets and requiring that the costs and quality of services be justified to users, causes an immediate decrease in discretionary costs. *Remember*—decreases in discretionary costs drop through and increase profits!

Financial Reporting on Research and Development Expenditures to Gain the Best Development Effort

Often research and development expenditures are loosely controlled. The firm does not receive the most from its research and development effort. Measuring the amount needed for research and development by an historical percentage of sales revenue is ineffective. The use of the percent of sales approach is acceptance of an inability to decide what amount of resources should be put into the research and development effort.

Like control in general, the control of research and development means a detailed and consistant application of sound business judgment. Each project which is assigned to research and development must be followed—in detail! The firm's managers must follow each project and evaluate the project's progress against the original objectives.

The report on research and development illustrated in this book is the catalyst through which managers evaluate, approve and modify the resources applied to research and development. The report on research and development, because it has all the necessary information, is the basis for evaluating each project and thus the total spent on each. Although the horizons of research and development are further away than for most other expenditures, these costs still require continual and detailed review by management as do all other costs.

Reporting for Control of Total Costs

Forecasting is not often thought of as cost control. But control implies a definition of objectives to control against. Control is not possible without a control criterion. Forecasting is the control criterion. Control begins with a forecast.

Forecast Reporting for Increased Profits

Control is achieved when the actual results equal or exceed the expectations in the forecast. Reporting of the actual results against the forecast tells management whether or not control is achieved. If the results are varying unfavorably from the forecast, the report will indicate where the variation is and managers can act to correct the deviation. Regardless of the course of action which management chooses, the report of the actual results versus the forecast will make the choice possible. Without the report, management would at best be guessing about what action is necessary. Profits can be maximized only when managers know where they want the firm to go and how it is progressing.

How Post Audit Reports on Financial Analyses Increase ROI

Although audit reports are sometimes thought of as historical information, they are an important and necessary control device. Particularly important are audits of financial analyses because they emphasize the results from internal decisions. Without this information managers would not know whether their decisions are correct or who is making the right (most profitable) decisions.

Audits of financial analyses are control through people because they measure the accuracy of a manager's decisions. If the decisions of some managers are continuously unprofitable, the audits will reveal this information and the firm's top managers must take corrective action.

Audits of financial analyses also measure the accuracy of the firm's forecasting and planning. There may be areas within the firm where forecasts are consistently inaccurate. The audits will disclose these areas.

Audits of financial analyses emphasize the variations from projections. Control is achieved through recognizing and correcting the exceptions. If prepared on a timely basis, audits of financial analyses lead to better decisions and higher profits. These reports are invaluable sources of information for correcting poor decisions. Poor decisions cause a lower return on investment.

Reduced Costs, Better Planning and Solid Sales Programs from Distribution Sampling

Distribution sampling reports provide the information needed to act before changes occur in the firm's sales volume. Distribution sampling provides the answer to the question: What is happening in the market place? Before control is possible, this question must be answered.

From the reports on distribution sampling, objectives can be adjusted before the firm is in a loss position. Distribution sampling reports reflect the next period's actual. From these reports the firm's managers can make any necessary adjustments to maintain profits.

Reporting on distribution sampling results in lower costs because inventory levels can be matched to expected sales, thereby reducing inventory carrying costs. Additionally, the manufacturing schedule can be adjusted to the demand for the product, including inventories on hand. The result is lower manufacturing costs. Furthermore, the closer the firm's total activity to the demand for its product, the lower the costs of personnel turnover. And every dollar saved increases profits!

Monitoring Cost Reduction Programs to Offset Cost Increases

Cost reduction reporting lets management know whether the reductions needed to maintain profits are taking place. Not only do cost reductions lower product costs through material substitutions and use of alternative manufacturing methods, they usually also improve serviceability and lower service costs. From the cost reduction report, managers can decide what actions are necessary to improve profits.

The report also emphasizes those areas and techniques from which most of the cost reductions are originating. This information can be used to identify areas where more effort is needed to identify cost reductions. Reporting on cost reductions makes it possible for managers to set cost reduction objectives and monitor results. Through this report, managers can fine-tune the operating contribution to profits!

Summary

The reports illustrated in this book cover all of a firm's costs. They include manufacturing costs, marketing costs, and all general and administrative costs. Although the reports are designed for profit maximization if used together, cost savings in a particular area can be realized by using a report designed for that area.

The reports illustrated in this book are applicable to all manufacturing and for almost all types of products. The only necessary requirement for using them is a desire for profits!

INDEX

D

E

F

S

T

U

V

W

Z